The Vectis Connection

PETER NEWBERRY

An Airspeed 'Envoy', G-ACMT, gets a birds eye view of the liner Queen Mary in the Solent.

British Aerospace

Preface

There are many books covering the history of the Isle of Wight Railways and also a considerable number on the maritime links from sail through to the steamers and finally catamarans, hydrofoils and hovercraft, but as far as the author has been able to establish, there has been very little research on air transport services to the Island. Research disclosed that during the 1930's the intensity of the operations was very much greater than first realised and it was possible to fly to virtually every major city in Great Britain. This book is an attempt to put on record these pioneering efforts which operated with virtually no navigation and approach aids and yet despite these shortcomings very few flights were cancelled because of weather.

Author's note Due to the absence of the ½p, the conversion from pounds, shillings and pence to decimal currency has been rounded.

The author expresses his sincere appreciation to the following individuals and organisations for the help, information and photographs that was willingly given and without which this book could not have been written. In alphabetical order:

On the Island Roy Brinton; Phyllis Bulbeck; Andy Gilliam; Isle of Wight County Press; Isle of Wight Mountbatten Library; Isle of Wight Public Record Office; Roger McDonald; Henry Nobbs; the late Alan Parker; Barry Price; Anne Springman; Charlie Taylor; Ray Wheeler; John Woodford.

On the Mainland Air Britain; Chris Balfour; Civil Aviation Authority; Central Library, Gatwick; Croydon Airport Society; Neville Doyle; David Dunstall, Shoreham Airport Collection; Simon Escott, Portsmouth Aviation Ltd; David Francis, University of Portsmouth Library, David Gibbings, GKN Westland PLC; Pamela Guess, British Aerospace PLC Farnborough; Hall of Aviation Southampton; John Havers, Colin Hendry Museum of Flight, East Fortune; Tom Hiett; Mike Hooks; Fred Huntley, British Airways PLC; Phillip Jarrett; John King; Morrab Library, Penzance; The News, Portsmouth; Diane Gregg and Sue Beresford, Portsmouth City Record Office; Peter Rogers; Tom Samson; Science and Society Picture Library, Science Museum; Southampton Central Library; Southampton Public Record Office; Arthur Tagg; Mike Tozer; Victor Turin, Barcelona; Ken Wakefield; Welsh Industrial and Maritime Museum; Maurice Wickstead; Hugh Yea.

Published by
Waterfront
A Division of Kingfisher Productions
The Dalesmade Centre, Watershed Mill, Settle, North Yorkshire BD24 9LR

ISBN 0 946184 90 9   Copyright Peter Newberry & Waterfront   December 2000
Publisher Roger Hardingham
Printed by The Amadeus Press, Cleckheaton, West Yorkshire

Contents

WEEK-END AIR SERVICE to the ISLE OF WIGHT from LONDON.

The Company proposes to inaugurate a Week-end Air Service from LONDON to the ISLE OF WIGHT, commencing at the beginning of June. The overall time of the Journey from the Centre of London to the Isle of Wight would be about 1½ hours, of which 50 minutes would be spent in the Air. The Company is desirous of discovering to what extent such a Service would receive the support of Residents of the Isle of Wight, and would welcome any suggestions as to the times the Service should leave London, on Friday or Saturday, and at what hour it should leave for London on Monday. Any suggestions would be welcomed and further particulars may be obtained from—   THE SECRETARY,
P.S. & I.o.W. Aviation, Ltd.,
Shanklin (Apse) Airport, Shanklin.

AIR FERRY between SHANKLIN and PORTSMOUTH

at any time by request. Fare—Single **15/-**, Return **27/6**.

PLEASURE FLIGHTS 5/-

Daily at Shanklin (Apse) Airport. 10 a.m. until dusk.

PORTSMOUTH, SOUTHSEA, & ISLE OF WIGHT AVIATION, Ltd.
Tel. Shanklin 324.

Pioneers & Pundits
the birth of commercial flight

Robert Loraine's forced landing on the Isle of Wight

Credit: Barry Price

It is fair to say that the Isle of Wight first came into prominence when Queen Victoria commissioned the alteration of Osborne House at East Cowes. This happened to coincide with the new steamship services and the expansion of the railways, with lines being built between all the major towns on the Island. These events attracted the gentility, but of greater significance to the Island was the influx of the rising middle class who tempted by the mild climate, bought and built houses mainly, but not exclusively, in Ryde, Cowes, Newport, Bonchurch and Ventnor. Newport was and still is the county town, but Ryde

and Cowes are on the north coast and therefore very convenient for the ferries to Portsmouth and Southampton respectively. Ventnor and Bonchurch, although on the south east coast, were easily accessible from the ferries as a direct railway line ran from Ryde Pierhead to Ventnor with train arrivals and departures being co-ordinated with the ferry sailings. The railways and steamship companies were very active in marketing the Island and offered "all inclusive" excursions to various events and places, Ventnor being sold for its mild climate and its bracing channel air. There was even a non stop train from Ryde pierhead to Ventnor and

Bleriot in the grounds of the Royal Spithead Hotel, Bembridge   Credit: John Woodford

called locally as the 'invalid express'! The result of this was that the Island became increasingly popular with holiday makers and the expanding resorts of Sandown and Shanklin catered for this influx.

The first recorded but unplanned cross Solent flight was on the 3rd August 1909 when Singer and Pollack lifted off in a balloon from Southampton, but during the ascent the northerly wind suddenly increased in strength and consequently they were blown across the water and landed at Cowes. The following day the wind had changed to south westerly and therefore they decided to take full advantage of this and once again successfully crossed the Solent, landing on the outskirts of Portsmouth.

Three days later the co-founder of the world famous firm of Rolls Royce, the Hon C.S. Rolls, filled a balloon with gas supplied by Cowes gasworks and duly launched it from a dinghy in the harbour; the winds must have been fickle as it took him two hours and thirty minutes to reach Lymington! C.S. Rolls was an early aviation enthusiast and was one of the founders of the Royal Aero Club, from which he received Aviators Certificate No 2 (Lord Brabazon held No 1). On the 2nd June 1910 he was the first pilot to make a non stop double crossing of the channel. In the following month he competed in the Bournemouth Rally piloting his Short built Wright "Flyer" which was a tail-less aircraft with the elevators out front. A few days before the event the

French licenced construction company issued a modification to fit the "Flyer" with a tailplane. Rolls ordered one from Shorts who built it exactly as depicted by the drawings but his mechanic was not impressed and distrusted the crude method of trussing. A test flight indicated that the increased longitudinal stability considerably reduced elevator effectiveness, but under pressure of competition, Rolls decided to overcome this by pivoting the new tail to act in unison with forward elevators. On the second day of the meeting a spot landing competition was held and Rolls, taking advantage of the gusting conditions, approached over the stands, entered a steep dive, and realising he was undershooting he pulled hard back which resulted, due to the increased bending load, in the failure of the fuselage structure. The machine then dived vertically twenty feet into the ground instantly killing Rolls. This was the first practical demonstration of stress multiplication due to suddenly applied loads. By this accident Rolls achieved the dubious distinction of being the first British subject to be killed in a heavier than air machine.

The 16th July was the last day of the pageant and a race to the Needles and back was organised, the actor manager, Robert Loraine entering as a competitor. The morning was cold and wet but nevertheless Loraine took off in his Farman (No 12) but ran into turbulent weather and was forced to land at Highdown, near Freshwater, Isle of Wight; thus becoming the first person to fly from the mainland to the

Island in a heavier than air machine. The organisers anticipating that a competitor might have to ditch set up what was probably the first air/sea rescue service. Page Croft M.P. and Sir Thomas Lipton positioned their yachts, respectively "Oriana" and "Erin" between Bournemouth and the Needles and waited for somebody to drop out of the sky! Back at Bournemouth and, in the absence of any news, concern was growing and Harry Harper, the Air Correspondent of the "Daily Mail" wired his paper with details of the "tragedy". This was later altered to praise Loraine's skilful landing on the Island! He returned to Bournemouth on Tuesday 21st July and reported a smooth flight. Loraine, who learnt to fly at Shoreham, then attempted a crossing of the Irish Sea on the 11th September by flying from Holyhead to Phoenix Park, Dublin, a distance of sixty miles. Unfortunately, not only was his Farman incorrectly rigged, which resulted in the flying wires snapping, but the Gnome engine was giving trouble and within sight of the Irish coast the engine completely cut, he managed to glide over Howth Head, thereby completing the sea crossing, but could not find a place to land, and with his Farman disintegrating, he ditched some sixty feet from the Bailey lighthouse and swam ashore. For this feat he was awarded the Royal Aero Club Silver Medal. During World War I Loraine served with the R.F.C. and was awarded the M.C. and D.S.O.

In late June 1911 a Mr Judd, proprietor of the Royal Marine Hotel, Ventnor, approached the Bristol Flying School with the idea of giving a display at the town. This was agreed and on the 5th July two Boxkites flew from Shoreham, one aircraft being flown by H.R. Fleming and Collyns Pizey, the other by Eric Gordon England who carried the luggage for all three. To guide them a beacon was lit on St Boniface Down and they landed successfully at Lawnfields, St Lawrence to a welcome of some 3,000 spectators and ships sirens in Ventnor Bay. On the Thursday demonstration flights were given but Fleming with a local butcher, Mr Burt as passenger, hit turbulent conditions which resulted in considerable damage. At the end of the meeting the other undamaged aircraft set up a new British record for passenger carrying by flying from Salisbury Plain to Brooklands, Rochester, Brighton, Ventnor, Salisbury and then home to Bristol, a total distance of some 350 miles.

During discussions by a committee of Ventnor residents relating to arrangements for the annual August Carnival it was decided to encourage an interest in aviation by inviting various pilots to give a display. One of the pilots who agreed to take part was Oscar Morison who had established a reputation for walking away from a number of crashes including a multiple cartwheel. On the 13th August he flew his Bleriot from Sandgate in Kent to Ventnor but suffered engine failure and was forced to ditch. The aircraft was

Robert Loraine's aircraft at Highdown   Credit: John Woodford

White No 2 Navyplane   Credit: Barry Price

Bristol Boxkite over Ventnor   Credit: John Woodford

Unknown early flying boat, believed to be at Gurnard

Sopwith/Saunders Bat Boat at Cowes
This aircraft was assembled at Cowes, the hull being of S.G. Saunders patented *"Consuta"* type which combined light weight with great strength.

salvaged and overhauled and was subsequently sold to W. Rhodes-Moorhouse, who was to become the first member of the Royal Flying Corps to be awarded a posthumous Victoria Cross.

Two others who agreed to take part were the above Gordon England and Collyns Pizey again flying Boxkites. It was their intention to arrive at Ventnor during the morning of the 14th but the exceptional hot weather combined with adverse winds prevented them leaving Larkhill, and it was not until the relative calm of the evening that they were able to depart. Pizey experienced engine problems and had to force land near the Horseshoe public house, Northwood, Cowes, but after allowing the engine to cool, he took off, but once again forcelanded, this time at Rowridge. The following morning he successfully made St Lawrence but upon landing a sudden crosswind carried him into the hedges. Gordon England fared little better by having to forceland after running out of petrol at Little Pan Farm near Newport, where Councillor Deacon invited him to stay the night. He took off next morning but crashed at Merston Cross, resulting in facial cuts and a broken nose. He eventually arrived at Ventnor in a cart! By this time the crowd were becoming frustrated but the day was saved by the arrival of

James Valentine, another British and Colonial pilot who gave a display in his Deperdussin, the first monoplane to land on the Island. According to the records the crowd were very impressed by his ability to climb to 2,000 feet! For the film "The Magnificent Men in their Flying Machines" a replica Boxkite, using the original drawings, was constructed and much to everybodies surprise it was found that the stress calculations of 1910 conformed to the current Civil Airworthiness regulations!

In 1911 the Government became concerned about the number of fatal accidents, as in the previous year there were 397 flights lasting over one hour out of which there were 29 deaths. During the first five months of 1911 the corresponding figures were 677 flights with 35 fatalities, thus causing the Government to introduce the Air Navigation Bill. As to why flights over one hour were specified as the criteria is not known! A more pertinent statistic was the fatality rate for all flights, irrespective of duration, of 8.2%.

In October 1911 a Boxkite *(No 19)* landed at Hayling Island flown by the Bristol pilot Howard Pixton with Lieutenant Charles Burney R.N. *(the son of Admiral Sir Cecil Burney)* as passenger. The objective was to carry out a number of over water flights, and although it is believed on one occasion it landed near Bembridge, it certainly flew along the east coast of the Island.

In August 1912 representatives of the Hendon based Graham White School of Flying visited Cowes with Graham White himself giving passenger flights in his Paulhan-Curtiss seaplane. Another of his pilots, J.L. Travers, operated joy riding flights in a Henry Farman seaplane. Graham-White, who was born at Bursledon, was one of the outstanding pioneer airmen, among his achievements was winning the Gordon Bennett Race at New York in October 1910. He was incensed by official indifference to aviation and was concerned that the French were forging ahead. To alert the public to this situation he had the words "Wake up England" painted on the fuselage of his aircraft.

On the 16th June 1913 two French aeronauts, Messieurs Dubonnet and Jourdan were found clinging to their balloon which had collapsed and descended into the sea south of the Island. They were picked up by a Dutch tug which landed them at Ventnor.

In 1912 the old established and famous shipbuilders J. Samuel White and Company Ltd of Cowes decided to enter aviation and engaged a Mr Howard Wright as General Manager and Chief Designer of their aviation department. This gentleman was a craftsman and self taught engineer who installed in 1907 a workshop under the railway arches at Battersea. He rapidly built up a business constructing aeroplanes to other peoples designs but subsequently graduated to designing on his own account and had a number of successful aeroplanes to his credit, among which was the first aeroplane for T.O.M. Sopwith. Their first aircraft was a failure but from the lessons learned they built a seaplane No 2 Navyplane.

It made a successful first flight on 23rd August 1913, with Eric Gordon England as the pilot who reported that it had a rapid take-off, an exceptional rate of climb and possessed first class manoevrability. The engine was a Gnome two row 14 cylinder rotary which produced 160hp. Many subsequent flights were made and a number of passengers carried including Howard Wright and Mrs Gordon England.

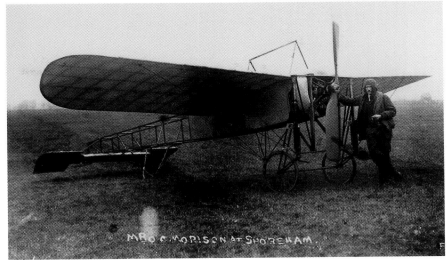

Oscar Morison with Bleriot at Shoreham   Credit: West Sussex County Library Service

On the 4th October the same year the aircraft was handed over to the Admiralty at Calshot for evaluation, the pilot being Lt. Spencer Gray who reported that it had easy handling qualities, with the design of the three step floats being particularly good. It was returned to J Samuel White's who carried out a programme of further testing including for a short period being fitted with a land undercarriage. On the outbreak of war in 1914 it was impressed by the Admiralty as number 884 and fitted with dual control. It was wrecked off Calshot in May 1915. Although this was a service aircraft its justification for inclusion is the fact that it crossed the Solent and therefore can be considered as one of the pioneers.

Replica Deperdussin   Credit: Steven Jefferson

in August 1914 the First World War broke out and to paraphrase Clausewitz, the object of war being "To impose one's will upon the enemy", there is obviously an over-riding incentive to develop better and more advanced technology than one's adversary, who is also doing likewise, it therefore becomes a race where normal peacetime commercial considerations are relegated to a lower priority. In 1914 both sides were equipped with low powered frail biplanes yet such was the speed of advance, a mere four years later Handley Page produced a four engine bomber, the V/1500 with a wingspan of 126 feet, a range of 1,300 miles and a maximum bomb load of 7,500lbs, a load not exceeded by a British production aircraft until the introduction of the Armstrong Whitworth Whitley!

During 1917 a Government Committee was set up under the Chairmanship of Lord Northcliffe, the Press Baron, "To consider the methods of regulating post war civil aviation activities. The Committee was a large one, consisting of forty members including Sir Sefton Brancker, the flying boat specialist Captain Porte, Brigadier Maitland who commanded the Military Airship Service and the futuristic writer H.G. Wells. In addition to the main Committee there were seven sub committees!

The report was submitted in February 1918, the bulk of which was naturally concerned with international matters such as Sovereign Air Space, Landing Rights, Bilateral Route Agreements and the establishment of an International Convention for Air Navigation -I.C.A.N. (the first I.C.A.N. was actually in 1910 but due to the war this was held in

*M. Salmets being greeted by the Chief Constable at Southsea Common
Southsea Common during his tour of the South. It is believed that he
landed on the Isle of Wight.*

Credit: Peter Rogers

C. Grahame-White and R.T. Gates in 1912

Credit: John Woodford

abeyance). Among the Committee's recommendations was that air transport should be developed to create a market for the aircraft industry and thus would be progressively able to design and build increasingly advanced aircraft. To support this aim a Government subsidy should be made available, at least until such time that air transport would be able to pay its own way. This view was strongly supported by Lord Trenchard, who had little interest in civil aviation, his motive being the preservation of the fledgling Royal Air Force from the predatory attitude of the other two services. He considered that an expanding and healthy air transport system would help with this aim. As we know he succeeded in preserving the R.A.F. but the Government flatly refused to grant any subsidy. A member of the main committee, a Frank Pick M.P. objected to the recommendation that the Air Ministry be the body responsible for controlling civil aviation on the grounds that the Board of Trade was responsible for the Merchant Marine and not the Admiralty and therefore the same should apply to its aeronautical equivalent but he was overruled.

Handley Page 0/400   Credit: Peter Rogers

On the 2nd January 1919 Lord Weir, Secretary of State for Air, and the wartime organiser of aircraft production, announced that draft legislation controlling civil aviation was being formulated, but nine days later in order to concentrate on his Scottish engineering business, he resigned. On the same day Major General Sir Frederick Sykes was appointed as Controller General of the Department of Civil Aviation *(D.C.A.)* which in turn was a department of the Air Ministry.

Boxkite at Hayling Island, 1911   Credit: Peter Rogers

On the 12th February a Bill was presented to Parliament embodying the main recommendations of Northcliffe, less the subsidy, by Winston Churchill the newly appointed Minister for War and Air, this becoming the Air Navigation Act 1919 and was granted the Royal Assent on the 27th of the same month. It was expected that civil flying would be authorised from 1st April but this was delayed as we were still technically at war with Germany and this would cause international complications. Potential operators of proposed internal services were incensed by this and in order to placate them the Government gave

permission for them to operate over the Easter period, with the Air Navigation Act finally being effective from the 1st May. On the previous day details were published of the Air Ministry's Air Navigation Directions *(A.N.D.s)* which set out requirements for Airworthiness, Registration of Aircraft, Overhauls, Licencing of Pilots, Navigators and Engineers, Rules of the Air etc. The first pilot to obtain a commercial "B" Licence was Flt Lt Saint and the first two licenced ground engineers were H.M. Woodhams and W. Kelly. Anticipating the Air Navigation Act the Daily Mail chartered a DH9 to carry newspapers from Hendon to Bournemouth, the aircraft crewed by Saint and Kelly, took off from Hendon at precisely 00.01 but ran into bad weather and crashed on Portsdown Hill on the outskirts of Portsmouth, Saint being seriously injured with Kelly

Avro 504 at Southsea, 1919

Credit: Peter Rogers

Avro 536 Seaplane off Sandown

Avro 504 at Southsea, 1919
This aircraft was operated by Island based F. Warren Merriam.

escaping with shock.

When the Great War ended there were very considerable supplies of surplus aircraft which came onto the market and a number of manufacturers including de Havilland, Handley Page and Supermarine decided to enter the air transport business and bought back from the Government their own products at about 25% of cost.

The first "commercial" flight to the Island took place on the 8th May 1919 when a Handley Page 0/400 bomber was chartered by the Daily Mail to parachute newspapers at various towns on the South Coast and to accommodate this the bomb cells were removed. As the flight progressed the newspapers were sorted into bundles by up to eight personnel, and therefore this must have been the first airborne sorting office! The aircraft, which was piloted by a Major Foot, arrived over Ryde at 08.00 with the intention of dropping the newspapers on Ryde pierhead but the windspeed was underestimated and they landed in the sea where they were picked up by a small boat.

July of 1919 saw further ventures with Captain Warren Merriam *(Aviators Certificate 179)* operating the prototype Avro 536 *(K-114)* seaplane at the Island resorts of Ryde, Sandown, Shanklin and Ventnor. The venture was obviously a success as in early August he was reinforced by an Avro 504L seaplane and both aircraft were intensively operated until the end of the month. Among other places bookings could be made at the offices of the "Isle of Wight Times", Union Street, Ryde with flights being advertised as "From One Guinea" *(£1.05).*

Supermarine Sea Eagle at Seaview

Frederick Warren had started his career in his father's saddle and harness making business, but later met an American O. L. Merriam who was interested in collecting historical literature and they formed a partnership at Falmouth as book and antique dealers. In 1901 he changed his name by deed poll to F. Warren-Merriam, but for what reason is not known. He married in 1904 but in 1909 his wife died leaving him with three children. He learnt to fly with Bristols at Brooklands and received his Aviators Certificate on 6th February 1912, going on to achieve fame as one of the their most reliable and successful instructors. In 1912 Edward Hotchkiss, the Chief Instructor, and Warren Merriam carried out 300 instructional flights in seven days and the following year when Merriam was Chief Instructor, he and his assistants trained only nine candidates short of the total of the sixteen other flying schools. On the outbreak of war in 1914 he was rejected by the R.N.A.S. due to poor eyesight but was offered a post as a civilian instructor. The Admiralty later waived the eyesight test but after a crash he was discharged, the cause being put down to his sight. He then re-applied, passed the medical, and flew Short 184 seaplanes on anti submarine patrols! He was demobilised in 1919 and worked for Avro's as a pilot in their joy riding business. When the boom ended he took up, like hundreds of others, chicken farming at Whiteley Bank near Shanklin.

During the 1914-18 war Supermarine of Woolston were contracted by the Admiralty to build a number of A.D. Flying Boats *(Admiralty Design),* and after the cessation of hostilities the company was successful in purchasing ten boats which had been in storage and therefore had not seen active service, for a very low price. In May 1919 it was decided to modify five of these aircraft to carry four passengers and as the ultimate intention was to operate a Southampton - Le Havre service, the 160hp Beardmore engine was replaced by the more powerful 200hp Hispano-Suiza.

They started operations from Woolston in July of that year with flights to Bournemouth and Southsea but on the 30th they carried a number of passengers who had missed the ferry at Southampton to Cowes, but why the ferry was missed is not known. During the same week, which happened to be Cowes Week, a number of charters were operated on behalf of people who wished to see the yacht racing from the air. Charters were also offered from Southampton to Cowes and it is known that these were very popular with yachtsmen and their guests who wished to travel to Cowes in the shortest possible time. On the 16th August they commenced operations to and on the Island and carried out joy riding from Ryde, Sandown, Shanklin and Ventnor, these activities were obviously reasonably successful as they carried on until late September, when they ceased the Isle of Wight operations and concentrated on the Le Havre services. One flying boat returning from France on the 29th experienced fuel shortage and alighted in Bembridge harbour, whereon the pilot, H.C. Biard went in search of petrol and was told "Its out of season!" He was eventually successful and completed his journey to Woolston. Three of these flying boats that operated in the Solent area have been identified as G-EAED (ex N1529), G-EAEE (ex N1710) and G-EAEK *(ex N1711).* The type was later named the "Channel" and were exported to a number of countries.

Kittiwake   Credit: GKN Westland PLC

In 1919 the Air Ministry issued a specification for a twin engine civil amphibian and S.E. Saunders Ltd of Cowes submitted a design. The resultant aircraft had a wingspan of sixty eight feet and was powered by two 200hp ABC Wasp II seven cylinder radial engines, the aircraft being named "Kittiwake" and registered G-EAUD. An innovation was a camber changing mechanism which caused the entire leading and trailing edges of the wing to move and was activated by a system of chains, push rods and worm gears. The leading edge flaps were so designed that when they were in the droop position they would produce an unbroken aerofoil, the trailing edges being conventional and in this position it was estimated that the stalling speed would be a low as 40mph. The theory behind this configuration was that it produced a double camber (patented by Howard Wright in 1912) and thus be more efficient across the whole of the speed range. When this was tested at Farnborough against a standard R.A.F. 6 aerofoil it was found that there were certain lift benefits but these were almost completely annulled by increased drag. Constructional problems caused the Kittiwake to be too late for the Air Ministry competition but Saunders carried on and it was first flown on the 19th September 1920 by Captain Norman MacMillan. At 600ft part of the starboard lower leading edge flap tore away causing a violent yaw, but fortunately the corresponding flap on the port side also became detached and in this condition MacMillan considered the stalling speed would by high and therefore made a fast speed approach and landing. Modifications were carried out but the Kittiwake did not fly again until March 1921, this time in the hands of F. Warren-Merriam. The Kittiwake was underpowered and it was scrapped after an R.A.F. pilot who was

unfamiliar with its unusual features crashed it off Cowes.

In 1921 the Brompton Motor Company applied to operate air services from Southsea Common but on the 19th April Portsmouth Corporation rejected their application and as a consequence they moved to the Island and offered joy riding facilities from a number of fields. the aircraft employed were de Havilland 6's registered G-EAWT, G-EAWU and G-EAWV, but their performance must have been marginal as they were underpowered being fitted with an 80hp Renault engine. The operation was later taken over by Martin Aviation Ltd, but its success is doubtful as by the autumn of 1922 their activities on the Island had ceased.

In September 1923 Sir Sefton Brancker, Director of Civil Aviation, flew Lord Apsley to Seaview, Isle of Wight, in the prototype Supermarine Sea Eagle G-EBFK. The purpose of the trip was to demonstrate the flexibility and comfort of the Sea Eagle and this it proceeded to do by taxiing up the beach. Another operator that carried out joy riding in the Island was Southern Counties Aviation Ltd but they were only present during the 1925 season and utilised a number of Avro 504K's.

Warren Merriam, despite his chicken farming, could not keep away from aviation and in 1922 he collaborated with G. Newman, the Works Manager at S.E. Saunders Ltd in designing and building a 36ft wingspan glider called the Merriam-Newman Glider. This was entered in the Daily Mail meeting at Itford in October (entry No 18) but due to faulty launching technique it crashed, Merriam being unhurt. The glider was reported at Godshill still in an airworthy

Medina

Credit: GKN Westland PLC

condition in 1930. It was later converted to a two seater and used at the Merriam Cowes based gliding school where complete courses were offered at a cost of £25. In 1926 Merriam opened what is believed to be the World's first aeronautical employment bureau, but apart from an unsuccessful venture in a gliding school at Cowes (Somerton), this was his swansong in active civil aviation. The employment bureau must have been a success as an advertisement appeared in "The Aeroplane" in 1939 for tradesmen. During World War II he joined the Fleet Air Arm in a non-flying capacity as a Lieutenant Commander based at Lee-on-Solent. he died in 1956.

Reverting to 1925 and in response to an Air Ministry specification for a new flying boat suitable for the Imperial Airways Empire routes S.E. Saunders Ltd produced the A4 Medina, its competitor being the Supermarine Swan. It was an unusual sesquiplane in that the upper wing was of lesser span than the lower, 52ft and 58ft respectively, with the dihedral only on the outer section of the upper wing. It was designed to carry two crew and seven passengers, being powered by two Bristol Jupiter VI eight cylinder radial engines and fitted with a variable incidence tailplane. The Medina was allocated civil registration G-EBMG and although faster than the Swan, maximum speed 115mph against the Swan's 92mph, no orders were forthcoming and it was scrapped in 1929. The probable reason as to why the Swan was preferred was that the hull of the Medina persistently leaked and was prone to impact splitting. Up in Brough, Yorkshire, the Blackburn Aircraft Company Ltd had produced a successful all wood light touring biplane featuring side by side seating and named "Bluebird". They manufactured four marks of this machine, the final version,

the Mark IV, was of all metal construction but as Blackburn's had just signed a contract for fifteen Baffin Torpedo bombers plus the conversion of sixty two Blackburn Ripons to Baffins, they had no spare capacity for the production of Bluebirds. Saunders Roe and Blackburns had a common majority shareholder, namely Whitehall Securities Ltd and to keep it in the family Saunders were contracted to build sixty five Bluebird IV's. the wings were built by Boulton and Paul of Norwich but every other component and completion was carried out at Cowes. An Hon. Mrs Victor Bruce was shopping in London when she saw a Bluebird in Selfridges for £550 in the window and bought it. She decided she would embark on a solo round the world flight but she would first have to learn to fly! While learning she had the Bluebird modified with an overload tank on the port side of the cockpit and the fitting of a W/T transmitter which automatically sent out a signal every fifteen minutes on 35.1M. She also installed a dictaphone so that she could record the progress of the flight. Mrs Bruce qualified for her "A" licence and with only 40 hours in her log book set off from Heston on the 27th September 1930 in Gipsy II powered G-ABDS *(also known as Bloody Daft Stunt),* the sixth aircraft to be built at Cowes. Her itinerary was Munich, Vienna, Belgrade, Istanbul, Konia, Baghdad, Bushire, Jask, Karachi, Jodhpur, Calcutta, Rangoon, Hanoi, Hong Kong, Amoy, Shanghai, then 600 miles across the Yellow Sea to Seoul and on to Tokyo where she arrived on the 24th November. The Bluebird was then loaded on the "Empress of Japan" and landed at Seattle on the 17th December. She then flew to Vancouver, San Francisco, Los Angeles and New York. The Bluebird crossed the Atlantic on the "Ile de France" arriving in le Havre on the 15th February 1931. She flew to le Bourget and then via Lympne to Croydon. On the

Dornier X at Cowes

Employees of Saunders Roe on a sponson of the Dornier X

following day she returned to Heston where the welcoming party consisted of just about every Bluebird in the country. Although repairs were carried out at various points the flight was virtually fault free but she became very concerned when en route to Hanoi as she was above cloud over high ground and not sure of her position. After dictating a final message in the dictaphone she commenced the let down, but with beginners luck, she broke into the clear over the railway line to Hanoi, where upon arrival was awarded the "Order if the Million Elephants and the White Umbrella."

Production of Bluebirds reached four per month but only fifty five were produced as the final ten were built at Blackburns, who by this time found their Military contracts running down. The largest single customer was National Flying Services who ordered twenty five, the first six of which were delivered from Cowes in formation on the 14th

Avro 504k G-EBQR at Bembridge, circa 1925

Meteor

Credit: GKN Westland PLC

F. Warren Merriam with Merriam-Newman Glider

January 1930. These aircraft were registered G-AAOA to G-AAOF and were painted in an orange and black colour scheme. Several of the Cowes built achieved fame and this was particularly so with G-ABDS, belonging to the Hon. Mrs Victor Bruce, her Bluebird was being on public exhibition during the last week in March at Charing Cross.

Another of the Cowes aircraft was Hermes II powered G-AAVG (No 33 built) which was piloted by Lt. Commander G.A. Hall on a leisurely flight to Australia. He departed Croydon on the 8th August 1932 and arrived in Wyndham twenty four days later. He would have made it in twenty one days but was held up in Burma searching for some lost aviators.

An unusual visitor to the Island was in June 1928 when Cierva C8L Autogiro flown by A.H. Rawson landed on the beach at Seaview. At the time this Autogiro was engaged in a 3,000 mile tour of the British Isles. In September of the same year it flew to Paris and was thus the first Autogiro to cross the Channel. It was then transferred to Cierva's French licencees, survived the War and is still extant the the Musée de l'Air, Paris.

In 1928 Sir Alliot Vernon Roe sold his Avro company to Hawker Siddeley Ltd and looked around for a suitable investment. In the November agreement was reached with S.E. Saunders Ltd and by December the company was reconstituted as Saunders Roe Ltd (Saro for short). S.E. (Sam) Saunders was by then 71 years of age and made Life President. Sir Alliot brought with him Harry Broadsmith who was appointed General Manager and Chief Designer. He also appointed John Lord as Joint Managing Director with himself.

The first aircraft produced by the new company was the Cutty Sark, a small (wingspan 45ft) flying boat/amphibian,

de Havilland 6

Credit: British Aerospace PLC

the design work commencing in March 1929 with the prototype, registered G-AAIP, completed in four months. This example was unusual as, unlike production aircraft it was not fitted with the Saro patented corrugated hull construction. Accommodation was provided for two crew in side by side seating plus two passengers and as a safety precaution the hull was divided into five watertight compartments. The well tried Avro/Fokker wing consisting of two box spars with plywood skinning was fitted and had sufficient buoyancy to keep the aircraft afloat if the hull was flooded. To avoid spray the two 105hp Cirrus Hermes engines were mounted on pylons which were also designed to take alternative power plants. Its first flight was on the 7th July 1929 and in the following month went to M.A.E.E. Felixstowe for certification *(test no: 555)*, receiving its Certificate of Airworthiness on the 31st August. In order to improve performance, in 1931 it was fitted with two close cowled 120hp Gipsy II's and so equipped it set off for a European sales tour, covering some 3,000 miles without any significant problems. It was then bought by Campbell Shaw and Tommy Rose who operated it on the Isle of Man Air Service between Liverpool and Douglas.

From aircraft number seven all remaining Cutty Sarks, except one, were fitted with 140hp Armstrong Siddeley Genet Majors, the odd one out being G-ABUF which was equipped with a single Armstrong Siddeley Lynx IVC of 240hp, and was the subject of a special order from Japanese pilot Yoshiharra for a flight from Vancouver to Japan, but was wrecked by him before setting out. A number of Cutty

Sarks were sold to Air Service training Ltd at Hamble where they proved ideal for converting pilots to the techniques of flying boat handling. In all twelve were built, the last survivor G-ABBC was destroyed in an air raid on Cowes in May 1942.

In 1929 Whitehall Securities Ltd formed a subsidiary known as the Aircraft Investment Corporation, the function of which was to provide finance for British civil aircraft projects and the famous racing driver Sir Henry Segrave was appointed Technical Director. Sir Henry wished to attempt to break the World waterspeed record and at the same time help in the design of a twin engine light touring aeroplane; both designs being entrusted to Saro. The boat named "Miss England II" was designed by Fred Cooper, and fitted with two 1,750hp Rolls Royce "R" type engines of Schneider Trophy fame. Fred Cooper later resigned to set up on his own as a power boat designer and in 1936 designed the "Bluebird" for Sir Malcolm Campbell who broke the World waterspeed record at a speed of 130.9mph.

The aircraft was designated the A.22 and named the Saro/Segrave Meteor, the construction was all wood with accommodation for four seats, power being provided by two 120hp Gipsy III engines. It went to A & A.E.E. in June 1930 who criticised it on the grounds of its inability to fly on one engine due to "excessive rudder forces and a propensity to enter an immediate spin at the stall". Despite this, it was granted with a Certificate of Airworthiness and was flown by Flt. Lt. R.L.R. Atcherley *(later Air Marshal Sir Richard)*

Cierva C8L Mk II G-ABYY at Seaview, May 1928   Credit: John Woodford

Three local ladies in front of Prototype Blackburn Bluebird III G-EBWE at Sandown   Credit: John Woodford
Centre: Mrs Nellie Blyth with sister Dorothy Woodford on right. Lady on left is a friend

Hon. Mrs Victor Bruce's Saro Windhover G-ABJP "City of Portsmouth"
off Clarence Pier, Southsea   Credit: Peter Rogers

Hon. Mrs Victor Bruce's Saro Windhover G-ABJP "City of Portsmouth"   Credit: "The News" Portsmouth

In 1932 the prototype Meteor was cannibalised to provide spares for the two Blackburn built aircraft. In the meantime Sir Henry Segrave carried out test runs in "Miss England" at Lake Windermere on the 13th June 1930 and achieved a speed of 98mph. On the following day he decided to break the record but almost at the end of the run he hit a floating log and was killed. The death of Sir Henry combined with Blackburn concentrating on the Military, and Saro on the Cloud prevented development of the Meteor.

In November 1930 the Dornier X flying boat visited Cowes. At that time this was the largest aircraft in the world with an all up weight of 105,820lbs, a wingspan of 157 feet and powered by Twelve Seimens built Bristol Jupiter engines each with an output of 525hp *(later twelve 600hp Curtiss Conqueror engines)*. Employees of Saunders Roe could view the Dornier by paying 6d for a trip on the company launch.

The relative success of the Cutty Sark encouraged Saro to build a larger flying boat/amphibian and designed on the same structural principles such as the Avro/Fokker wing, pylon mounted engines, and the conventional Saro metal hull. It was named the "Cloud" and had

and Flt. Lt. G.H. Stainforth, both of the R.A.F. Schneider team, in the Kings Cup Air Race but were forced to withdraw due to starboard engine trouble. Blackburn's of Brough were given a contract to build two modified versions, these having a metal fuselage and the wings placed further aft. The first Blackburn built aircraft G-ABFP was tested at A & A.E.E. in March 1933 (test No: 566A) who stated that it was much improved but assymetric handling was still interesting! The prototype G-AAXP was demonstrated to General Balbo of the Italian Air Force who was so impressed with it that two were ordered and built under licence by Piaggio.

a wingspan of 64ft, the prototype being registered G-ABCJ. accommodation was provided for two crew plus six to eight passengers. The prototype was tested at M.A.E.E. Felixstowe in July 1930 *(test report: 571)* and was powered by two 300hp Wright Whirlwind engines, it receiving its Certificate of Airworthiness on the 1st August, and was sold to Canadian Captain Robert Hall as CF-ARB. In January 1934 it was repurchased by Saro for experimental purposes and fitted with two Napier Rapier IV 16 cylinder H type engines each producing an output of 340hp. It was then leased to Jersey Airways but was withdrawn from use in 1936.

The second civil Cloud was G-ABHG and was a special order from the Hon. A.E. Guinness who christened it "Flying Amo". It was initially powered by three 215hp Armstrong Siddeley Lynx IVC seven cylinder radial engines but before delivery was refitted with two Pratt and Whitney 425hp Wasps, it was unique by having three fins and rudders, two in the conventional position and one small one beneath the tailplane. It was the only Cloud to have an auxiliary aerofoil fitted above the the engines, the object being to improve elevator response at low speeds but it is doubtful if this had any significant effect as it was later removed. The Hon. A.E. Guinness paid £9,000 for this aircraft while the R.A.F. only paid £5,000 for their Clouds! In 1939 it was sold to Imperial Airways for pilot conversion purposes, its Certificate of Airworthiness expiring in May 1941. It was not considered worth renewing it was used as a rest centre for the staff of B.O.A.C. In 1952 the hull was discovered being used as a caravan at St Leonard, near Ringwood, Hampshire.

The third civil Cloud was registered G-ABXW "Cloud of Iona", obtained its Certificate of Airworthiness in July 1932 and then sold to British Flying Boats

Saro Cloud fitted with 340HP Armstrong Siddeley Servals   Credit: Barry Price

Saro Cloud G-ABCJ fitted with 340HP Napier Rapier IV engines   Credit: Barry Price

Ltd for a service between Stranraer and Belfast. When this company ceased trading it was sold to Guernsey Airways. On the 31st July 1936 it took off from St Peter Port, Guernsey with a total of ten occupants but disappeared en route to Jersey, the wreckage being found on rocks two days later; the enquiry blamed an air lock in the fuel system.

The last civil Cloud was G-ACGO which received its Certificate of Airworthiness in July 1933 and powered by two 340hp Armstrong Siddeley Serval ten cylinder air cooled radials, these engines being for all practical purposes a double mongoose. It was despatched on a European sales tour and it impressed the Czech State Airline

Ceskoslovenske Statni Aerolinie *(CSA)* to such an extent that they bought it, the only stipulation being that two 300hp Walter Pollux engines be fitted. It was delivered in July 1934 and operate through to 1939. During the German occupation it was stored, but after the liberation the wings could not be found and therefore the hull, less the tail, was put into service as motor launch "Delfin", it being used in this form on the Ultava until the mid 1960's. Recent information is that it is currently being restored to flying condition. A total of twelve Clouds were built but eight were for the Royal Air Force and as the subject is civil aircraft details of these are not relevant.

*Junkers A50 Junior after forced
landing on the Island. Believed to be G-AATH*

Credit: Henry Nobbs

Saro was pleased with the sales of these two types of aircraft and therefore it was decided to build two more amphibians of intermediate size. Two aircraft were built and named "The Windhover" with a wingspan of 54' 4", power being provided by three 120hp Gipsy II 4 cylinder air cooled in line engines. The Windhover was designed for a maximum of eight occupants, the first one was intended for export to New Zealand as ZK-ABW for use by Dominion Airways, but this fell through and was sold to Matthews Aviation PTY of Hobart, Tasmania as VH-UPB. From January 1933 it operated the Melbourne - King Island - Launceston route but on 14th May 1936 it was wrecked off King Island, Bass Strait.

The second aircraft G-ABJP was utilised for handling trials, during the course of which it was discovered that with engines off, elevator control became sluggish. To rectify this an auxiliary winglet was fitted which improved the airflow over the tail; the penalty being increased drag. Upon completion of the trials it was sold to Gibraltar Airways for the Gibraltar - Tangier route and named "General Godley". It completed 117 return flights before being bought by the Hon. Mrs Victor Bruce for an attempt on the World endurance record. In order to prepare the Windhover, she flew with Captain S.D. Scott and S.G. Ford to Gibraltar, and on the following day (June 1st) they took the Windhover to Alicante where they stayed overnight. On take off the following morning all three engines failed, the aircraft being badly damaged in the subsequent landing. It was then dismantled and shipped to Cowes where it was repaired, named "City of Portsmouth" and modified with three extra fuel tanks, namely a 75 gallon tank in the mainplane, and 84

and 75 gallon tanks in the hull. A wind driven fuel pump was installed and to augment this handpumps were also fitted. A R.A.F. Flight Lieutenant was nominated as Captain and depending on which report is read he was a navigation, meteorological and engineering specialist! A catwalk on the wing was fitted and a safety harness was made available as the poor Flight Lieutenant was expected to carry out in-flight engine maintenance! In-flight refuelling was scheduled for three times in every twenty four hours and was performed by a unique method in that a modified Bristol Fighter *(G-ABXA)*, "Mercenary Mary" and a D.H. Moth would take off with a length of cord attached to each aircraft. At the rendezvous the Windhover would fly between them, pick up the cord, sever the piece attached to the Moth and haul in the length from the Bristol Fighter, at the end of which was the fuel line. The first attempt was from Clarence Pier, Southsea, but failed when after two hours they had to return for various adjustments to be made. Another attempt was made achieving a duration of 15 hours 40 minutes but due to fog they lost contact with the tanker, resulting in water landing in thick mist off Ventnor at 06.00 hours. The Bembridge lifeboat received a call to search for an aircraft in distress but this was cancelled as a launch belonging to Spencer Bros of Ventnor put out. The crew were taken ashore and given breakfast by Mr Arthur Rowe, Chairman of Ventnor Council and afterwards Mrs Victor Bruce spent a good hour signing autographs. A final attempt was made remaining airborne for 54 hours 13 minutes but again were forced to return, this time due to excessive engine temperatures. Mrs Bruce stated in an interview with the Portsmouth Evening News that the record attempt had cost her £7,000 which was a very considerable sum of money, as in 1932 a respectable

Island Flying Club's Prototype General Aircraft Cygnet G-AEMA at Sandown, 1936   Credit: Henry Nobbs

detached house would have cost in the region of £500. The Windhover was then sold to Jersey Airways with which it operated until withdrawn from use in 1938.

Although Cowes *(Somerton)* airfield *(also known as Northwood and by the R.A.F. as West Wight)* had been in use since 1916, first by J. Samuel White Ltd and then Saunders Roe Ltd, there was little commercial activity as operators preferred the more populated east Wight area and the first "real" airport on the Island can be considered as Shanklin *(Apse)*. It was opened in the summer of 1929 on land which was part of Apse Manor Farm and was owned by a Mr and Mrs T. Fiske. The operator was Inland Flying Services *(later renamed Wight Aviation Ltd and subsequently Portsmouth, Southsea and Isle of Wight Aviation Ltd)*. They initially operated Avro 504K's but in 1932 and became the first company to offer a genuine scheduled service to the Island.

Spartan Aircraft Ltd which originated as Simmonds/Spartan became an associated company of Saro Ltd both companies being majority owned by Whitehall Securities Ltd. They produced a number of designs including the Arrow, the three Seater, the Clipper and three different marks of the cruiser, details of which are set out in the chapter on this company.

The prototype Spartan Three Seater G-ABAZ "Island Queen" was sold to Charles Coombs of Shanklin Flying Service. It won both the Nottingham and Yorkshire Air Races held on the 13th and 14th September 1930 at speeds of 102mph and 98mph, the pilot being Lt. Col. L. Strange who had become a director of Spartan.

In 1932 Portsmouth, Southsea and Isle of Wight Aviation Ltd began looking for a larger site than Apse and in February bought part of Barnsley Farm on the outskirts of Ryde *(now partly occupied by Tesco)*. This was to be named Ryde Airport and was to develop into the Island's major air terminal. The first genuine scheduled service to the Island commenced on the 27th June 1932 from Portsmouth to Ryde and was flown by PSIOWA's brand new three motor Westland Wessex which initially operated a four times daily service in each direction. In April the following year another airline started operations from Cowes to Heston and return twice daily. The operator concerned was Spartan Airlines which was owned by Spartan Aircraft Ltd.

On the 10th May 1929 the Royal Assent was granted to the railways *(Air Transport)* Bills of 1928/29 and this empowered the railway companies to enter into this new form of public transport. They formed a company known as Railway Air Services Ltd and on the 30th July 1934 they started a twice daily service between Birmingham and Cowes, via Bristol and Southampton using de Havilland Dragons. The Island was now served by three airlines, Spartan being subsequently merged with other airlines on the mainland and became a component of British Airways, the Island operations ceasing in 1936. In the same year, however, Channel Air Ferries commenced a service between Shoreham, Bembridge and Bournemouth and this continued until they merged with Great Western and Southern Airlines Ltd.

Air transport was now expanding throughout the country and in July 1933 the Government set up a committee under the chairmanship of Lord Gorell to examine and recommend the regulation of air operations. The outcome was the setting up of the "Air Registration Board" which was duly incorporated into the Air Navigation Act of 1936.

In 1935 the Island Flying Club was formed at the new airport of Sandown (Lea) and became very active; more details of this will be found under the section covering this airport.

In July 1935 the government set up another committee under Brigadier General Sir Henry Maybury, the brief being "To consider and report upon measures which might be adopted for assisting the promotion of civil aviation and the requirements of the Post Office for Air Mails and the relationship between aviation and other forms of transport". The committee held twenty three meetings and reported in December 1936 but meanwhile another committee known as the "Cadnam Committee" was investigating the workings of Imperial Airways but were given wider terms of reference.

Until 1938 anybody could start an airline and provided they observed safety standards they were free to operate where they wished, but the outcome of the Maybury and Cadnam reports was the establishment of the Air Transport Licencing Authority. On the 23rd June 1938 an order in council under the Air Navigation Act 1936 stated that on the 16th September the Air Navigation *(Licencing of Public Transport)* order would become law and that all operators had to submit applications for permission to operate various routes. In respect of the Island the following services were granted:-

Portsmouth, Southsea and Isle of Wight Aviation Ltd
    Portsmouth - Ryde
    Bournemouth - Ryde
    Portsmouth - Sandown
    Southampton - Ryde

Great Western and Southern Airlines
(owned by Great Western and Southern Railways who also incorporated Channel Air Ferries into G.W. & S.A.)

1 Liverpool - Manchester - Birmingham - Bristol - Southampton - Ryde - Shoreham
2 Shoreham - Ryde or Bembridge - Bournemouth - Bristol - Cardiff - Exeter
3 Shoreham - Ryde - Bournemouth *(local)*
4 Heston - Croydon - Bembridge *(on demand)*

In December 1938 a White Paper *(CMD 5894)* gave details of proposed subsidies to internal airlines. To a total of £100,000 with a maximum of £10,000 to any one company the formula was:-

6d *(5p)* per ton/mile for year one decreasing by ½d in each of years two, three and four and 4d *(1.6p)* in year five. The scheme was designed to last for five years but the war intervened and therefore these arrangements went by the wayside.

What was it like to fly in those days? Apart from the natural fear and apprehension of committing oneself to a form of transport that defies gravity and whose only means of support was the air itself, it was in many ways more relaxing than today. It was possible to book a scheduled flight through a travel agency or at a railway station but it was more likely that one would call at the local office of the airline, which in many cases was little more than a kiosk. There were such kiosks on the piers at both Ryde and Southsea. One could of course telephone a booking but it was only the financially comfortable who could afford such an instrument. There were no credit cards in those days and having decided to book a flight one would either pay in cash or by cheque. There were also no cheque guarantee cards and anybody who possessed a cheque book was considered to be socially acceptable, honest and trustworthy.

Upon arrival at the aerodrome, which was little more than a large grass field, one checked in at the 'terminal' which was normally a hut-like structure, the sole purpose of which was to check your tickets *(no computers)* and be weighed, the latter sometimes being to the embarrassment of the ladies! This was essential as the aircraft were relatively low powered and passengers plus their luggage must not exceed 200lbs. If the flight was not full then excess baggage would travel with you, but if not it would have to wait until a flight which had sufficient capacity to forward it. Having had your ticket punched or torn and had been weighed, the whole process taking about a minute or so, you and your fellow passengers, which were normally less than ten, were escorted to the aircraft *(no security checks)* and sat in the first available seat. There being no flight attendants, the pilot would tell everybody to strap in and then start the engines and taxi out over usually very bumpy ground. He would then run up the engines to check the magnetos, temperatures and pressures and when satisfied he would line up on the 'runway'. There was no question of being delayed by air traffic slots as air traffic control was minimal and if it existed at all it consisted of a chap who would flash red or green on his Aldis Lamp. In respect of the runway this was a grass strip aligned to the prevailing wind and to reduce rolling resistance the grass was cut shorter than the rest of the field. When ready the pilot would open up the engines to full power, and the aircraft would rapidly gain speed, accompanied with considerable cabin noise and vibration, which once airborne would settle down to more comfortable levels. Passengers would sometimes be given a map which showed places of interest along the route which was useful as the aircraft flew at between three and four thousand feet and therefore it was easy to pick out landmarks. The pilot navigated by the aid of maps, and this being before the Clean Air Acts, there were plenty of smoking chimneys from which it was possible to indicate not only the direction of the wind but by the angle of smoke to the ground an estimate of its strength. Another aid to navigation was the practice of large railway stations painting their name in large white letters on the roof.

As the flight approached its destination the pilot would throttle back the engines which then gave a slow rumbling sound and then land on another grass strip that was similar to the one at the aerodrome of departure. Upon leaving the aircraft first time passengers would have feelings of both relief and exhilaration, the exception being small boys who were full of excitement and wanted to go again!

Finally, the following appeared in "The News" Portsmouth and is reproduced with their kind permission. Although this has nothing to do with the Isle of Wight it well illustrates the vagaries of pre-war flying.

One of the strangest flights to land at Portsmouth must surely have been the small biplane carrying eight Welsh miners on their way to a rugby international. They had left Cardiff on a murky February morning in 1934, bound for Edinburgh, where Wales and Scotland were due to meet. Thick fog in the Midlands, however, forced their pilot to turn back, only to find that Bristol Airport was also out of action. Undaunted, the miners instructed the pilot to put them down anywhere that they could watch a decent football match. Discovering that Portsmouth was fog-free, the party promptly landed and found themselves at Fratton Park watching Pompey play Sheffield United. When a reporter caught up with them in a hotel later that evening, he described them as "eight of the happiest disappointed men I have ever seen".

Portsmouth, Southsea & Isle of Wight Aviation Ltd

Previously Inland Flying Services Ltd and Wight Aviation Ltd

Note: This company changed its name on four occasions. For the sake of accuracy and to avoid any misunderstandings, the dates quoted are those of the dates of approval by the Registrar of Companies. It will be appreciated that there is a time lapse between a name change being decided by the Board of Directors and the date of approval by Companies House. It is illegal to trade under a new name until such sanction has been obtained.

Klemm L.27 III G-ABJX of PSIOWA

de Havilland 60X Moth of PSIOWA.
When operated by Portsmouth Aero Club, this aircraft crashed in the sea at Spithead on 7th November 1934, both occupants killed.

In early 1929 a Captain R.M.B. Ward and a Mr A.B. Forsyth agreed to form a company to operate in the field of aviation and on the 6th April that year a company was incorporated and named "Inland Flying Services Ltd", its base being Maylands Aerodrome, Romford, Essex. The nominal capital was £2,500 in £1 shares and the registration number was 238,470. In the previous year Maylands was an unlicensed landing ground and was used by British Flying and Motor Services Ltd for Joy Riding purposes employing an AVRO 504K G-EBSJ. Inland Flying Services successfully applied to the Air Ministry for a licence to operate Maylands Aerodrome and, armed with this, commenced negotiations with the farmer owner for a three year lease on the Aerodrome. These did not come to fruition, as during the summer season of 1929, a better opportunity presented itself at Apse Farm, Shanklin, Isle of Wight. The Island had a history of involvement in aviation and included such pioneers as J Samuel White Ltd and S.E. Saunders Ltd. Inland Flying Services therefore considered that the population was already air minded and the demand for various flying activities should be healthy, and with this in mind they acquired two Avro 504Ks G-AAFE and G-AAFT. Many thousands of these aircraft were built in a number of variations and from 1919 onwards a considerable number of war surplus 504s came onto the market. It also became the standard RAF elementary trainer from the end of World War I until replaced by the Tiger Moth in 1932. As the name suggests, Apse Farm Aerodrome was part of Apse Manor Farm which was owned by a Mr and Mrs Fiske. The first season was up to expectations but one of the 504s G-AAFE was becoming expensive to maintain and was withdrawn from use in early 1930, being replaced by a de Havilland 60X Moth G-AAAG. In order to reflect more accurately it's association with the Isle of Wight the company decided to change it's name to "Wight Aviation Ltd", this being registered on the 1st May 1930. During the peak of the season Wight Aviation, in order to satisfy demand, chartered Mr Coombs prototype Spartan Three Seater, G-ABAZ "Island Queen". Operated by Mr Coombs "Sandown and Shanklin Flying Services" until transferred to the Island Flying Club in 1934 with whom it served until the outbreak of war in September 1939. It survived the war, the registration being cancelled in December 1946. At a board meeting held on January 15th 1930 Mr AB Forsyth resigned and the Chief Flying Instructor Mr WL Woodward was appointed in his place. On the 30th April 1930 Wight Aviation formed the "Isle of Wight Flying Club" the directors being the above Mr Woodward and a Portsmouth solicitor Mr AG Murray who was also a director of the parent company. Incidently, before the club was officially formed the above Mr C. Coombs, later of Sandown and Shanklin Flying Services, was trained and was the recipient of the first Island awarded "A" licence. In regard to the licence held by the company in respect of Maylands Aerodrome, Romford, one can only assume

that it was sold or transferred to Edward Hillman of Hillman Airways who subsequently made Maylands their main base.

The company's mainstay was the de Havilland Moth G-AAAG, the aircraft that became almost standard equipment for flying clubs around the country as it was the first considered robust enough to stand up to the constant rough treatment of the clubs and schools. The result was that the Moth was an instant success (first flight 22nd February 1925) and impressed even the Air Ministry who sanctioned

Lionel Balfour Credit: Chris Balfour

Lionel Balfour with DH 60G Moth G-ABJH Credit: Chris Balfour

Lionel Balfour's Puss Moth G-ABIY   Credit: Chris Balfour

was registered in the name of A.G. Murray he was probably a nominee, a not uncommon practice in those days. These aircraft were later joined by a new Isle of Wight built Spartan Three Seater G-ABLJ, this latterly being mainly based at Apse. Another aircraft on the scene at that time was L.M.J. Balfour's D.H. 60G Moth G-ABJH but in May 1932 it was sent to the Spartan works at Cowes for a complete overhaul and emerged repainted in the livery of PSIOWA.

In the same year Mr L.M.J. Balfour, a director, flying a Puss Moth G-ABIY in the 1931 King's Cup Air Race held at Heston on the 25th July, achieving a very respectable fourth place. Although this aircraft remained his personal property it was used to supplement the company's fleet until March 1935 when it crashed at Ryde. In 1931 Lionel Balfour was certainly very active in aviation sporting events and in addition to the above he participated in the Grosvenor Cup race at Newcastle on the 22nd August. He was the first to arrive in the London - Paris - Cannes Aerial Rally on the 7th September and ironically the second aircraft to arrive was Lionel Balfour's own Puss Moth G-ABIY flown by Cathcart Jones. Later in the month he came second in a spot landing competition at the Bristol Air Pageant and on the 3rd October he competed in the London - Cardiff Air Race which was part of the opening celebrations of the new airport at Cardiff (Splott). Balfour's sister Rachel won a Puss Moth in a raffle which he took over. In 1931 he won the National Flying Services Club draw for a passage in the Graf Zeppelin's British tour but sold the ticket!

subsidies for certain favoured flying schools. Many hundreds were built and the basic concept spanned many variations such as the Cirrus Moth, Gipsy Moth, Metal Moth etc. Production lasted nearly ten years and at its peak de Havilland were producing three a day. Concurrent with this production the manufacturers were designing a successor which became the most famous Moth of them all, namely the Tiger Moth, which became the standard trainer of the Royal Air Force and was also exported to twenty five countries. By the time the war ended in 1945 over 8,000 had been built.

1931

The season opened with Wight Aviation possessing two aircraft, which were the Moth G-AAAG and a Klemm L27AIII. The latter was a German built light aircraft but in this case powered by a British 95HP Cirrus engine. The L27AIII version was a three seater with accommodation for two passengers in the front cockpit. Although this aircraft

1932

In late 1931 the company decided that joy Riding held an uncertain future and with the forthcoming designs of new economic aircraft such as the de Havilland 84 Dragon, the Westland Wessex and the Spartan Cruiser it was decided to operate a ferry service from Portsmouth to the Island, research having shown that some 2,500,000 people crossed the Solent every year. Shanklin *(Apse)* not being entirely suitable for such aircraft a new site had to be found and after considering a number of possibilities they were successful in March 1932 in obtaining the freehold of 82 acres of Barnsley Farm for a consideration of £12,000. This site was situated to the immediate east of the main Ryde-Shanklin-

Sandown road and only one and half miles from the town centre.

While this was going on the company was completely re-organised, the original directors having resigned. The board now consisted of: L.M.J. Balfour, Flt Lt F.L. Luxmoore DFC, Capt F.S. Symondson MC and A.G. Murray. During World War I Francis Luxmoore served on the Western Front with 46 and 54 Squadrons and disposed of four enemy aircraft before being shot down and made a prisoner of war. When the war ended he remained in the newly formed Royal Air Force and was posted to Mesopotamia *(now Iraq)*, serving with Number 1 and 45 Squadrons. On becoming tour expired he was awarded the D.F.C. and then resigned from the service.

The Company's capital was increased to £17,500 and a chief Pilot was appointed, a Mr JHA Wells. As it was the intention to operate from the new airport at Portsmouth the name of the company was changed once again, this time to "Portsmouth, Southsea and Isle of Wight Aviation Ltd". This new name must have been the longest in the British Civil Aviation Register and it was ironic that another South Coast transport operator also had the longest name in the Shipping Register, namely, "Southampton, Isle of Wight and South of England Royal Mail Steam Packet Company Ltd" *(now shortened to Red Funnel)*. This change of name was approved on the 11th May 1932.

HRH The Prince of Wales inspecting PSIOWA Wessex G-ABVB   Credit: GKN Westland PLC

PSIOWA's specially modified Wessex   Credit: GKN Westland PLC

PSIOWA's Wessex G-ABVB. Note later colour scheme   Credit: GKN Westland PLC

In 1928 the Air Ministry wrote to all towns and cities with a population of over 20,000 advising them of the desirability of establishing Municipal Airports. Portsmouth City Corporation had been considering this and they called in the well known airport consultants M/s Hunters of Chester, the main works being carried out by local contractor Frank

Bevis. The airport was operational from 1931 but was not officially opened until 2nd July 1932. The opening ceremony was performed by Sir Philip Sassoon, Under Secretary of State for Air, and attracted over 100 aircraft and in excess of 50,000 visitors. Displays were given by Hawker Furies of No 1 and 43 Squadrons and Tiger Moths of the RAF's

Pilots of PSIOWA
Left to right: A.L. Upton, C.R. Crow, E. Ellison, A.W. Whitta, R.C.W. Ellison, H.G. Lines

Credit: Chris Balfour

Central Flying School. Other aircraft included an Armstrong Whitworth Argosy, a Westland Pterodactyl plus many and varied light aircraft.Having access to airports on both sides of the water, Portsmouth, Southsea and Isle of Wight Aviation Ltd *(in future referred to as PSIOWA)* commenced negotiations with Portsmouth City Council, agreement being reached on the 12th April 1932. This gave PSIOWA sole rights to provide Joy Riding, Air Taxis, Air Tours, a scheduled service to the Isle of Wight, and the sale of petrol. In return for these sole rights the company agreed to pay the City 17.5% of all gross takings but in the case of the proposed scheduled service no payment to be made for the first year ending 25th March 1933. The company rented the then largest hanger at the airport for a period of five years at a rent of £250 PA for the first two years, £300 for the third year and £350 for years four and five. The City appointed Mr J.H.A. Wells, the chief pilot of PSIOWA, as ground engineer and Flying Control Officer responsible to the City Engineer. The City paid Mr Wells £2.00 per month for his services! In the meantime PSIOWA were talking to the various aircraft manufacturers about a suitable passenger aircraft and after various negotiations and delivery dates they settled upon a Westland Wessex.

The Wessex was a three engine high wing monoplane powered by Genet Major engines

PSIOWA's DH 84 Dragon G-ACRF over Ryde Pier Credit: Andy Gilliam

Rolls Royce crash wagon

each of 140 HP. The routes of PSIOWA were of very short duration and therefore subject to far greater number of landings and take offs than usual. Working together PSIOWA and Westland agreed certain modifications to lengthen the life of the Wessex including wings with Duralumin spars instead of wood, a strengthened undercarriage, accommodation for up to nine passengers and the Pilot's cabin raised above the wing for improved visibility. It was delivered on 6th May 1932 and cost in the region of £3,000, the registration being G-ABVB. This particular Wessex was the only one to be cleared by A and

A.E.E. Martlesham Heath (test No 524D 5/32) for a maximum take off weight of 6,300lbs; previous Wessex aircraft were criticised by A and A.E.E., despite being fitted with brakes, for a long landing run; the reason for this was the brake lever was out of reach of the pilot! Although the Wessex proved to be a good workhorse, it was overshadowed by the economics of the de Havilland 84 Dragon which had the same passenger capacity but was powered by only two engines. The Wessex was painted in the new livery of PSIOWA with a blue fuselage with blue registration letters in a biscuit colour panel. The division

Monospar ST-4 G-ABVN approaching Southsea

between the colours was lined out in red. The wings and tailplane were doped aluminium.

Services commenced to Ryde on the 27th June 1932 with four flights per day in each direction and in the first six weeks some 1,700 passengers were carried. The fares were: 6/- *(30p)* single and 10/- *(50p)* return. Children under twelve were carried for 3/- *(15p)* and 5/- *(25p)* respectively. Free surface transport was provided from Portsmouth City Centre and from Ryde Airport into town.

From July, in conjunction with Solent Coaches a through London *(Victoria Coach Station)* to Ryde was offered at 12/- *(60p)* single and 23/- *(£1.15)* return. A day return was also available at 17/6 *(87p)*. At weekends and Bank Holidays the fares were increased by 1/- *(5p)* single and 1/6 *(9p)* for returns. The free baggage allowance was 30lbs *(14kg)*.

Commencing the 25th August 1932 a "Round the Island" sightseeing flight was introduced departing Portsmouth at 17.00 and calling at Ryde and Shanklin, the flight time from Portsmouth being one hour and from Shanklin 45 minutes. The fares were from Portsmouth 39/6 *(£1.97)* and from Shanklin 29/6 *(£1.47)*. It was advertised as following the coastline all the way, so that the best views were obtained of Bembridge, Culver Cliff, Sandown Bay, Luccombe, Dunnose Head, Ventnor, St Catherine's Point and lighthouse, Freshwater Bay, the Needles, Alum Bay, Totland Bay, Hurst Castle, Cowes, Osborne House, Wootton Creek and Ryde.

Traffic continued to build up on the Portsmouth-Ryde ferry and the frequency of services were increased. To satisfy

demand it was obvious that an additional aircraft would be necessary and the company was fortunate in acquiring the prototype general aircraft four passenger Monospar ST-4 G-ABVN. This aircraft was a twin engine low wing monoplane powered by two 85 HP Pobjoy R engines and was designed by Mr HJ Steiger. Steiger had earlier developed the "Monospar" construction, comprising of a single Warren girder spar which combined light weight with high resistance to bending loads, resulted in a wing of great strength. It has been claimed that this aircraft could from a standing start, take off on one engine *(on 85 HP?)*.

On the 5th September a new route was commenced from Shoreham to Portsmouth and Ryde. this was initially flown once per day in each direction but was later increased to two. The Monospar normally worked the route but, when demand was heavy, Mr L.M.J. Balfour's Puss Moth was utilised as an additional aircraft, the service being later extended to Shanklin. Southern Aircraft Limited managed Shoreham Airport and PSIOWA operated the route in conjunction with them.

Pleasure flying was carried out at Portsmouth, Ryde and Shanklin at 5/- *(25p)* per person with longer flights as required. The aircraft involved were the Klemm G-ABJX, the Moth G-AAAG and the Spartan 3 Seater G-ABLJ.

The Portsmouth-Ryde ferry continued to maintain its popularity but if the advertised schedule did not suit the requirements of potential passengers they could simply telephone for an aircraft to take them across the water at any time. The fare for this service was 15/- *(75p)* single and 27/6

Fox Moth of PSIOWA   Credit: Mike Hooks

Fox Moth of PSIOWA   Credit: Mike Hooks

the Fleet Earl Jellicoe G.C.B. O.M. G.C.V.O. L.L.D. D.C.L., who after retiring from the Royal Navy, lived at St Lawrence.

In the Channel Island of Jersey the Chamber of Commerce were investigating the possibility of an airport and invited Mr Balfour to act, in effect, as a consultant. He visited a number of sites and produced a report within twelve days. He hoped that PSIOWA would be appointed consultants for the planning of the airport and also that he might obtain rights to open an air service from Portsmouth. Although PSIOWA had applied to be placed on the Air Ministry Approved List they had not been accepted by the date for the selection of consultants and although approval came through

(£1.37) return. Mr Lionel Balfour, a director of PSIOWA, extolled the virtues of air transport quoting speed and convenience, and although he had a vested interest he certainly practiced what he preached as he commuted from his Island home every day, thus reducing his journey time to fifteen minutes as opposed to the normal rail/sea/rail which took up to two hours.

Mr Balfour had a significant family connection on the Island in that his wife, Lady Myrtle, was the daughter of Admiral of

shortly afterwards, the Deputy Director of Civil Aviation at the Air Ministry, a Mr Bertram, rejected their submission, despite the fact that he must have known that they were about to be accepted.

The first year of scheduled operations was very satisfactory and, in particular, the Ryde ferry had exceeded all expectations, having carried 3,400 passengers in the first nine weeks. Consolidating both the scheduled services and Joy Riding a total of 15,418 passengers were carried by the kiosk on Shanklin seafront.

In 1933 PSIOWA formed Portsmouth Aero Club but prior to this they were approached by Sir Charles Rose, a young man with a desire for a career in aviation and who was prepared to invest £3,000 in the company. Lady Rose, Sir Charles mother, wrote to Lionel Balfour requesting his opinion and to his credit he gave the honest reply that such an investment would be highly speculative.

end of the financial year. During the winter of 1932/33 the Ryde ferry was operated at four per day in each direction and the Shoreham-Portsmouth-Ryde service at twice daily. Extra services were operated according to traffic demands.

During late 1932 Mr G.E. Eckersley-Maslin was appointed Chief Pilot.

1933

On April 10th 1933 the Portsmouth - Ryde service increased to twelve times daily, including Sundays, from the 16th May an extra evening service operated, departing Portsmouth at 20.10 and Ryde at 20.20. The fares were 6/- *(30p)* single and 10/- *(50p)* return. For children under twelve they were 3/- *(15p)* and 5/- *(25p)* respectively. Six flights from this service continued on to Shanklin which was advertised "Also for Ventnor", at 10/6 *(52p)* single and 19/6 *(97p)* return. Passengers joining at Ryde could take the short hop to Shanklin for the cost of 6/- *(30p)* single and 10/- *(50p)* return. Also, from April 10th, the Shoreham-Portsmouth-Isle of Wight service operated at thrice daily including Sundays. The flight time between Shoreham and Portsmouth was twenty minutes and the total elapsed time between Shoreham and Shanklin *(including stops at Portsmouth and Ryde)* was fifty minutes.

The fares were:-

	single	return
Shoreham - Portsmouth	12/- (60p)	23/6 (£1.17)
Shoreham - Ryde	14/6 (72p)	27/6 (£1.37)
Shoreham - Shanklin	19/- (95p)	37/- (£1.87)

Air Taxis were available from Ryde to other Island destinations; for example, the fare to Cowes *(Somerton)* was 16/- *(80p)* for one passenger and 20/- *(£1.00)* for two *(50p each)*.

PSIOWA booking offices at Portsmouth were at the City Airport, the Portsmouth Aero Club and kiosks at Clarence and South Parade Piers. On the Island there were offices at Ryde and Shanklin Airports, 61 Union Street, Ryde, and a

Sir Charles later become very active in the affairs of Portsmouth Aero Club which became a separate limited company in 1935 and by 1937 he was Managing Director. At one time he owned 60G Moth G-AAKN and it has been suggested that he and Luxmoore jointly bought it in June 1932 and operated it at Portsmouth Aero Club. This is doubtful as the Club was not formed until May 1933 and it is significant that the Moth was not registered to him until April of that year. On 21st July 1934 F.L. Luxmoore flying G-AAKN was the winner of the Portsmouth Trophy Race. In August of the following year the Moth was sold to Airwork Ltd, but was bought back by Portsmouth Aero Club in June of 1936 who operated until October when it crashed at Farlington mudflats, Langstone Harbour.

Due to the demand on capacity PSIOWA decided to acquire two de Havilland Fox Moths. This was a single engine biplane powered by a 130 HP Gipsy Major engine and a wingspan of 30' 10½". Early in 1932 Mr A.E. Hagg, Chief Designer of the de Havilland company had set out to design a light transport offering first class economy and performance combined with low capital cost, the result being the Fox Moth. In order to reduce manufacturing costs the Fox Moth utilised the wings, tail unit, undercarriage and engine mountings of the Tiger Moth. All the above were bolted to a new fuselage which could carry up to four passengers in an enclosed cabin with the pilot in an open cockpit, although about a third of the production had a sliding hood. It was ideally suited for short sectors and, as C.G. Grey, Editor of "The Aeroplane", stated it was "Unquestionably the first British aeroplane to support itself financially in the air". The Fox Moth was an outstanding success and made money for its operators. A total of 98 were built, of which 52 were exported. In 1946, some fourteen years after this little biplane first flew, the de Havilland company of Canada produced their own version with an uprated Gipsy Major engine of 145 HP, selling some 52 in Canada, Southern Rhodesia, India and Pakistan and only ceasing production when they started to build Chipmunks. At the time PSIOWA acquired their two Fox Moths the price for a standard model was £1,045. The two were registered G-ACCA and G-ACIG, the latter remaining with the

Scene at Portsmouth in the early 1930's. Aircraft are: Moth G-ABJH, Puss Moth G-ABIY,
Klemm L27 III G-ABJX. Fox Moth G-ACIG, Wessex G-ABVB is taxiing for take off.   Credit: Chris Balfour

company until impressed in the RAF in 1940. They were used primarily on the Portsmouth-Ryde ferry but they also worked the Shoreham routes and were the favoured aircraft of the company for joy-riding. One was chartered to fly three passengers to Jersey.

A Portsmouth-Ryde-Bembridge service was introduced with the latter being on 30 minutes request. Passengers transferred to another aircraft at Ryde, this extension being very popular during the holiday season owing to the fact that Bembridge Airport was within a mile from Whitecliff Bay. The return to the mainland was accomplished by passengers telephoning PSIOWA and requesting an aircraft to pick them up. The fares from Portsmouth were 9/6 *(47p)* single and 16/6 *(82p)*. Childrens' fares were 6/6 *(32p)* and 11/- *(55p)* return.

PSIOWA approached Portsmouth City Council requesting more frequent bus services from the City centre to the Airport. The Council refused and, in response to PSIOWA's suggestion that they operate their own, it informed them that Public Service Vehicles with a capacity of eight or more passengers would require a local authority licence which would not be forthcoming! To overcome this the company purchased two secondhand limousines which had a maximum capacity of seven passengers.

The Monospar ST-4 G-ABVN was sold at the end of the year. Interestingly, this aircraft disappeared from all records

until its fuselage was discovered at Bankstown, Sydney, New South Wales in 1954.

During the winter of 1933/34 the Shoreham-Portsmouth-Ryde-Shanklin route terminated at Ryde with two services per day. Charters were offered to the Grand National and a scheduled service operated between Ryde and Goodwood during race meetings.

The 1933 traffic returns showed a healthy increase over the previous year but whereas in 1932 a large proportion of passengers were taking flights for pleasure, in 1933 the opposite was true which was a good omen for the future. The figures for the period 2nd June to 28th September showed passengers carried on the Portsmouth-Island routes were 6,827, an increase of 100%.

The "Round the Island" sightseeing flights continued with the same fares as in 1932. In 1933 the Chief Pilot was still G.E. Eckersley-Maslin who later joined Jersey Airways in a similar capacity. He had a long life, dying in Tasmania aged 96.

1934

At the end of 1933 PSIOWA and Portsmouth City Corporation commenced negotiations for the revision of the original 1932 agreements, the outcome of which was that PSIOWA relinquished their monopolies to their various

PSIOWA's Dragon G-ACRF at Christchurch.

Credit: Allen White/Laurence Hayward Collection

activities at Portsmouth. The new agreements confirmed the right, but not the sole rights, to operate scheduled services to the Isle of Wight for a period of 21 years, the percentage payment of gross receipts to the Corporation being reduced from 17.5% to 10%. The same percentages applied to air taxis, petrol and third party servicing but the company retained the sole rights to joy-riding, the fees for this being 15% of gross receipts.

These arrangements were to the benefit of both parties as on the one hand it reduced PSIOWA's operating costs and on the other it left Portsmouth free to talk to other potential operators such as Jersey Airways and Railway Air Services. During the 1930s Portsmouth's main employer was HM Dockyard and therefore the economy of the City was virtually dictated by the Admiralty. To reduce this reliance the City was active in trying to attract other industry and in this connection was successful in concluding a deal with Airspeed *(1934)* Ltd. During the next few years Airspeed expanded considerably and by the beginning of 1939 employed 1,800 people. They were the designers and builders of the Airspeed Oxford of which 4,411 were built at Portsmouth alone. One of the directors was Neville Shute Norway (Neville Shute the novelist) and a plaque on a house in Helena Road, Southsea, commemorates his time at Portsmouth.

In 1933 an experimental air service was started by the Great Western Railway between Plymouth and Cardiff and from the very first flight mail was carried. Overlooking the special relationship the railways had with the GPO, other airlines erroneously took this as a green light and started to carry mail and issued their own stamps.

PSIOWA were not slow off the mark and in January 1934 issued special stamps which depicted a Westland Wessex flying over Portsmouth Guildhall, an initial run of 4,000

were printed perforated on two sides only. The stamps were endorsed with consecutive serial numbers in red and were sold in books of twenty, a second run of the same quantity were printed but these were perforated on all sides. Despite being warned by the Postmaster General that the carriage of mail was illegal, PSIOWA flew twenty covers in each direction between Portsmouth and Ryde on the 8th February. In the meantime the Postmaster General was impressed with the service offered by Railway Air Services and therefore, on the 24th July 1934, he announced that he was prepared to utilise other carriers. the result was that PSIOWA and other airlines incorrectly interpreted this as clearance and produced further stamps. These depicted an aeroplane flying over the Needles and were produced in both blue and sepia, the blue being intended for mail outbound to the Island and the sepia on the return flight, but in practice the stamp nearest to hand was used. PSIOWA were again informed that this was illegal but carried on. As late as December 1934 a letter was posted in Ryde using PSIOWA stamps and surprisingly this was accepted by Ryde Post Office, flown to Portsmouth, cleared at Mount Pleasant and then carried to Australia on the first Air Mail Service by Imperial Airways and Quantas Empire Airways!

To replace the Monospar sold in December PSIOWA ordered a new de Havilland Dragon G-ACRF, the agreed delivery date being May 1st. On this date it was intended to start a new route with this aircraft, namely London (Heston) - Ryde - Shanklin, but due to delays in receiving its Certificate of Airworthiness it was not delivered until the 18th. It was configured to carry eight passengers but by utilising the baggage area up to ten could be carried. The Dragon was equipped with a Marconi AD6 radio, the first PSIOWA aircraft to be so fitted. Between the 1st May and the delivery of the Dragon the London - Island route was worked by the Wessex G-ABVB. At the London end passengers booked in

Courier painted in PSIOWA original scheme

advance and checked in at Victoria Coach Station, the cost of surface transport to Heston and from the Island airports to the nearest town being included in the fare. The route was actively marketed as the "Island Air Express". On the same day *(May 1st)* their competitors Spartan Airlines Ltd, trading as "Southern Air Services", also restarted their London - Island service, this time from Croydon. Due to their association with Railway Air Services they had an advantage over PSIOWA as would be passengers could book at the majority of the larger railway stations. Their fares were £1/10/0 *(£1.50)* single and £2/10/0 *(£2.50)* return to either Ryde or Cowes with Bembridge on request, surface transport at both ends being inclusive. While in the planning stage of this new route PSIOWA realised they were at some disadvantage but against that the Dragon had lower operating costs than the Spartan Cruisers, having only two engines instead of three. This enabled PSIOWA to announce lower fares at 19/6 single *(97p)* single and 38/6 *(£1.93)* return, thus undercutting Spartan by 10/6 *(53p)* and 11/6 *(58p)*

respectively. These fares were equivalent to the monthly First Class rail fare. A passenger leaving London Victoria would arrive at Ryde one hour twenty minutes later and at Shanklin in an additional ten minutes. The actual flight time from Heston to Ryde was forty minutes, the free baggage allowance being 30lbs. Excess baggage cost 3d per pound.

The frequencies of the route were as follows:-

1st-16th May	
Twice daily in each direction	*One on Sundays*
17th-23rd May	
Six times daily	*Four on Sundays*
24th May-30th June	
Three times daily	*Two on Sundays*
1st July-31st Aug	
Six times daily	*Four on Sundays*

There were no services on May 20th, 21st or August 5th and

6th. The handling agents for PSIOWA at Heston were the British Air Navigation Company and booking facilities were also available at Grosvenor House, Park Lane and London Coastal Coaches, Victoria Coach Station. Booking facilities on the Island were now available at:-

Ryde	The Airport
	61 Union Street
	Happy Landing Cafe
Seaview	The Double H
Shanklin	The Airport
	Summer Arcade
	Regal Theatre
Ventnor	Nash's Garage
Cowes	Fountain Garage

For the summer season commencing 25th June the Heston - Island route carried both the London Evening News and the London Evening Standard, the carriage of London papers being suspended at the end of the season on 31st August. On the subject of newspapers, from 1933 the 'The News' Portsmouth was flown to the Island on a regular basis and this continued post war *(but not by PSIOWA)* until the introduction of the Hovercraft. The aircraft used was the Fox Moth which would leave Portsmouth with the early afternoon edition and then call at Ryde, Bembridge, Sandown, Shanklin and Cowes. In mid winter the Fox Moth had to be back in Portsmouth before dark and therefore this involved a very tight schedule.

Between May 17th and 30th June a Ryde-Bournemouth route operated twice daily, increasing to four times daily from July 1st, two of which connected with Western Airways under the "Sunshine Air Express" scheme
(of which more below).

The Shoreham ferry operated as follows:-
From 24th March - 16th May
Ryde-Portsmouth-Shoreham Twice daily inc Sunday. From 17th May this service was re-routed as follows:- Shoreham-Portsmouth-Bournemouth *(connections at Portsmouth for Ryde and Shanklin).* This route was part of an arrangement with Western Airways which, as its name implies, served the West Country, from its base at Bristol *(Whitchurch).* This company was started by a Bristol man, Norman Edgar, who was a manager for Merlyn Motors Ltd which, in addition to cars, held a de Havilland agency. He later branched out on his own and in September 1932 started a Bristol - Cardiff service. This became successful and in order to expand and regularise matters he formed Western Airways Ltd in September of the following year with a capital of £7,500. Like PSIOWA the company developed other routes which in turn led to the joint marketing exercise named as "Sunshine Air Express". Passengers from Cardiff and Bristol flew all the way to the Island under this slogan, although at Bournemouth they changed from Western Airways, normally Dragon G-ACJT, to a PSIOWA aircraft.

Retractable undercarriage of Courier Credit: British Aerospace PLC

Retracted & Lowered **5,718** *Times in* **62** *days*

At Cardiff connections could be made to Plymouth, Birmingham and Liverpool. The connection was valid until 30th September when PSIOWA closed the two routes for the winter.

The fares to Ryde from:-
Bristol
34/- *(£1.70)* single   65/- *(£3.25)* return
Cardiff
43/6 *(£2.17)* single   82/6 *(£4.12)* return
Bournemouth
14/6 *(72p)* single   27/6 *(£1.37)* return

All the above were in addition to the well established Ryde and Shanklin ferries. Easter was early that year and on 29th March (the Thursday before the Easter weekend) the winter service was upgraded to a flight every thirty minutes between Portsmouth-Ryde-Shanklin and continued over the Easter period. The ferry then reverted to departures every hour until May 17th when it operated a thirty minute frequency until sunset throughout the summer to 30th September. Since inception the ferry had been an success and PSIOWA took the opportunity to reduce fares. The new fares being:-

		New fare	**Old fare**
Portsmouth-Ryde	Single	4/6 *(23p)*	6/- *(30p)*
Portsmouth-Ryde	Return	8/6 *(43p)*	10/- *(50p)*
Portsmouth-Shanklin	Single	8/- *(40p)*	10/6 *(53p)*
Portsmouth-Shanklin	Return	14/- *(70p)*	19/6 *(98p)*
Portsmouth-Bembridge	Single	8/- *(40p)*	
Portsmouth-Bembridge	Return	15/- *(75p)*	

Cheap day returns were also offered, subject to timing restrictions, as follows:-

Portsmouth-Ryde	5/6 *(28p)*
Portsmouth-Shanklin	11/- *(55p)*
Portsmouth-Bembridge	12/- *(60p)*

Airspeed Silver Jubilee airmail posted in Shanklin 7th May 1935 and signed by the pilot

The new fares generated more traffic and forced PSIOWA to charter extra aircraft during the peak period. These included two de Havilland Dragons and possibly an Avro Commodore, all from the British Air Navigation Company.

The "Round the Island" tour continued as in previous years and such was the popularity PSIOWA were able to reduce the fare to 29/6 *(£1.48)*.

All this activity required extra finance and therefore it was decided in April to increase the paid up share capital from £17,500 to £22,500.
In 1934 Portsmouth were playing Manchester City in the Cup Final at Wembley *(Portsmouth lost)* and on the 27th April the "Football Mail" was flown from Portsmouth to

Heston, Ryde and Cowes. The following day, which was the day of the match, the Wessex operated a shuttle service between Portsmouth and Heston at an all in return fare of 25/- *(£1.25)*. Surface transport from Portsmouth City Centre and to Wembley Stadium was included.

On the 24th June the Wessex was chartered by a group of eight to see the French Grand Prix. It left Bournemouth for Paris at 11.40 and returned at 21.25. On the 7th of the following month a

Airspeed Courier. Sir Alan Cobham's experiment!

Credit: British Aerospace PLC

Mr Kirby chartered an aircraft to take him from Cowes to Paris, leaving Cowes at 09.00 and returning at 19.00. The aircraft has not been identified but the pilot was R.C.H. Monk.

At the end of July a mobile radio was installed at Portsmouth. This was a low powered Bellini Tosi set operating on both W/T and R/T and with a D/F facility. It is understood that it suffered night error of some magnitude!

The Goodwood Races were held between 31st July and 3rd August and the Wessex was called upon to operate a shuttle service between Ryde and Goodwood. The return fare of 30/- *(£1.50)* included ground transport to the racecourse to and from Goodwood Airfield *(during the War this airfield was known as Westhampnett and was a satellite for Tangmere)*.

In the spring of 1934 the Air Ministry issued a NOTAM *(Notices to Airmen)* setting up an air traffic route between Portsmouth-Ryde and Shanklin. Service aircraft were requested not to overfly but RAF aircraft were regularly target towing for shore based guns and as this duty entailed flying at ninety degrees to the airway it was hardly avoidable. To complicate matters further, in October the Air Ministry declared a danger area from north east to due south of No mans land fort. The area was to be used for high altitude bombing and anything below 15,000 feet was to be considered in danger. Commercial aircraft flying at 1,500/2,000ft along the airway could ascertain as to whether the range was "live" by looking for a white arrow displayed on the roof of the fort!

During the winter of 1934/35 the Portsmouth-Ryde ferry was reduced to five flights each way, the London *(Heston)* service continuing to operate throughout the winter but at a much reduced level. There were two services on Monday mornings departing Ryde at 08.30 and 10.30 and departing Heston for the return flights at 09.20 and 11.20 respectively. There were no services on Tuesdays, Wednesdays and Thursdays but on Fridays there were three return flights, this being increased to four on Saturdays, leaving Heston at 09.20, 11.20, 13.20 and 15,20. During this winter the Shoreham - Island and Bournemouth services were operated on request with the stipulation of a minimum of two passengers.

1934 was a successful year with more than double the number of passengers than in 1933. According to official figures in "Report on the progress of British Aviation", published by the Air Ministry, the passenger total was 32,900 and mileage flown 288,000. These figures may well be understated as other sources indicate that the figures were in the region of 39,200. It is possible that the Air Ministry accidently transposed their figures in which case this would read 39,200 which ties in with other sources. This also questions the mileage flown; the writer believes the true figure should be about 350,000. During the August Bank Holiday PSIOWA achieved their largest uplift in a single day by carrying 1,019 passengers.

The free baggage allowance was still 30lbs with excess at the now reduced rate of 2d per pound, but with the over-riding stipulation that the combined weight of the passenger plus luggage must not exceed 200lbs. During the year Mr E.C.W. Ellison became Chief Pilot, replacing G.E.

Eckersley-Maslin who had joined Jersey Airways.

1935

In 1934 PSIOWA started planning for continued expansion to commence in 1935. The Wessex and the Dragon had been worked very hard and it was obvious additional aircraft would be needed. Fortunately they did not have to look very far as their neighbours at Portsmouth Airport, Airspeed, had a number of unsold Couriers of which three were leased, the registrations being:
G-ACZL, G-ADAX and G-ADAY.

Scene at Airspeed Courier G-ADAY about to depart from Portsmouth   Credit: Mike Hooks

Airspeed offered a choice of engines with the Courier, namely the 240HP Armstrong Siddeley Lynx IVc, the Armstrong Siddeley Cheetah V of 305HP or the Cheetah IX which delivered 350HP. The PSIOWA aircraft were fitted with the Lynx which was a seven cylinder air cooled radial engine enclosed by a Townend ring cowling which drove a metal two bladed propeller. The Courier was a low wing monoplane of very clean lines resulting in a cruising speed of 132MPH and as such was considerably faster than the Wessex or the Dragon and on short hauls it could accommodate a pilot and five passengers. During the design stage close attention was paid to aerodynamics but the Courier's greatest innovation was a retractable undercarriage operated by a hydraulic assisted handpump, the first British commercial aircraft to be so fitted. As such, the Courier was the first aircraft with a retractable undercarriage to be tested by A. and A.E.E. With the undercarriage in the up position, the climb to 5,000ft was improved by four minutes and the top speed increased by 30mph *(test No:-624 8/33)*. These were the days before undercarriage warning horns and the only indication of the position of the undercarrriage was a single light on the instrument panel, which upon closing the throttle was supposed to glow red. On one local flight Sir Alan Cobham, who had become Chairman of PSIOWA in 1935, forgot to lower the undercarriage which resulted in an unscheduled wheels up landing at Portsmouth. He came out with a story that he wished to test the theory that a wheels up landing would cause minimum damage to a Courier! PSIOWA promptly ordered that the undercarriage of their Couriers be

Credit: Mike Hooks

permanently locked down! The reason given that as they only operated on short sectors there was no real advantage to having a retractable undercarriage, but whether Sir Alan's mishap influenced this decision is not known. Although the Courier was of advanced design with the ability to carry five passengers it was more expensive than the Dragon and as a consequence only sixteen were built.

In 1935 PSIOWA acquired Westland Wessex G-ABAJ which was originally a Sabena aircraft but bought by Sir Alan Cobham's company, Cobham Air Routes. After the fatal ditching of another Wessex G-ADEW, Sir Alan sold his company to the Olley group who had no requirement for the Wessex and thus it came to PSIOWA. In May a new

Airspeed Envoy was acquired *(G-ADCA)*. This twin engine aircraft was designed basically on the same lines as its smaller stablemate, the Courier, and for fleet commonality purposes was fitted with the same Armstrong Siddeley Lynx IV engines. It was the first British commercial aircraft to be subjected to an official complete destructive test of the wing, a procedure which later became standard practice. The Envoy had the same passenger capacity as the Wessex but was 50% faster on only a little more power.

A high cruising speed coupled with such features as a retractable undercarriage and flaps attracted foreign buyers and envoys were exported to France, Czechoslovakia, India, South Africa, China and Japan, with ten being built under licence in the latter country. An Envoy was chosen for the King's Flight and registered G-AEXX, and was painted in the red, white and blue livery of the Brigade of Guards. A number of French Envoys went to Spain during the Spanish Civil War as did the PSIOWA Envoy G-ADCA in 1936. Not including the ten built under licence in Japan some fifty one Envoys were produced but at £4,500 it was expensive and it is doubtful if Airspeed made any significant monies from this design, but nevertheless it did form the basis for the Oxford which became the standard twin engine trainer of the RAF, some 8,586 being built.

The Portsmouth-Ryde ferry continued with its off season frequency of four flights daily in each direction but on the 18th April it was upgraded to a hourly service and from the 7th June the service was again increased to every thirty minutes commencing with the 09.10 from Portsmouth *(09.22 from Ryde)* until sunset. The fares were the same as in 1934, except for the cheap day return which was increased to 7/- *(35p)*.

The Portsmouth-Shanklin direct service operated at eight flights daily in each direction but unlike the Ryde ferry the fares were reduced to 6/6 *(33p)* single and 12/6 *(63p)* return, but against this the day return was increased slightly from 11/- *(55p)* to 11/6 *(58p)*. The cheap day returns were not available during the period 12th to the 17th July inclusive as 1935 was the year of the Jubilee Fleet Review at Spithead and additionally they were also not available during Bank Holidays.

A Southampton-Ryde-Shanklin route was inaugurated on the 10th April at an initial frequency of four times daily but from 7th July this was increased to five including Sundays. The fares were 7/- *(35p)* single and 13/6 *(68p)* return. Passengers travelling to Shanklin paid an extra 2/- (10p) and 4/- (20p) respectively and cheap day returns were available to Ryde at 12/6 *(63p)* and Shanklin 16/6 *(83p)*. Company cars conveyed passengers to Eastleigh Airport from 28 Cumberland Place in the City centre for a fare of 6d *(3p)*.

FLYING FROM THE ISLE OF WIGHT

RYDE AIRPORT.

PORTSMOUTH.   Frequent Services Daily.   FARES: From 3/6S, 6/-R
BOURNEMOUTH.   Seven Services Daily.   9/-S, 16/6R, 15/6DR
SOUTHAMPTON.   Four Services Daily.   7/-S, 13/6R, 12/6DR
The Flying Times are about 8 minutes, 15 minutes, and 10 minutes respectively.

COWES (Somerton Aerodrome).

SOUTHAMPTON.   Four Services Daily.   FARES: 5/-S, 9/6R, 8/6DR
The Flying Time between Southampton and Cowes is about 10 minutes.
SEA COACH/AIR EXCURSION to Southampton at 130 m.p.h. by cabin aeroplane, returning by Sea Coach at 25 knots.   RETURN FARE 8/6.

SHANKLIN (Apse Airport).

PLEASURE FLIGHTS OVER SHANKLIN PIER, 4/6, over SANDOWN AND SHANKLIN PIERS, VENTNOR, or RYDE, 7/6.
Free Car Service to and from Airport.

STEAMER AND/OR RAIL-AIR TICKET INTERAVAILABILITY.

Passengers holding the return halves of Ordinary, Monthly, or Week-end Rail and/or Steamer Tickets to BOURNEMOUTH, PORTSMOUTH, & SOUTHAMPTON from certain stations in the Isle of Wight, on payment of the appropriate supplement, may return by Air.

On the subject of ground transport the corresponding rates at other airports were as follows:

Portsmouth
From either South Parade or Clarence Pier 10 minutes and 15 minutes before departure time at a fare of 6d *(3p)*

Bournemouth
By company car free of charge from 77 Holdenhurst Road

Shoreham
By company cars from 25 Marine Parade, Brighton and Seafield Garage, Kingsway, Hove, both at a fare of 1/6 *(8p)*

London
Free of charge by Express Coaches from Victoria Coach Station, 164 Buckingham Palace Road, SW1 and Heston Airport

Shanklin Airport
From and to the airport from the following Island towns:

Shanklin	
Regal Theatre, High Street	6d *(3p)*
Ventnor	
28 Pier Street	1/- *(5p)*
Ryde Airport	
By Southern Vectis buses	4d *(2p)*
Sandown	
Southern Vectis buses	7d *(3p)*
Seaview	
Company car	
from Castleton & Rand, High St	6d *(3p)*
St Helens	
Company car	6d *(3p)*

Monospar ST-10 G-ACTS at Portsmouth. Prior to joining PSIOWA this aircraft won the King's Cup in 1934.

Credit: Chris Balfour

Reverting to the new Southampton route this provided a useful connection to other destinations as follows:
The 10.10 and 17.10 from Shanklin connected with Provincial Airways services to Torquay, Plymouth, Newquay and Penzance, the latter service connecting at Southampton with the Provincial Airways service to Leicester, Nottingham, Grimsby and Hull.

The Shoreham-Ryde-Shanklin ferry operated at four times per day with the 09.55 and 17.15 from Shoreham continuing onto Bournemouth to connect with the Western Airways to Bristol and Cardiff. The Island bound aircraft from Cardiff and Bristol departed Cardiff at 10.05 and 17.30, arriving at Shanklin 11.45 and 19.05. These two services then continued onto Shoreham with an intermediate stop at Ryde. Connections for Portsmouth for all those services was via the Portsmouth-Ryde ferry. As previously stated the route was marketed under the banner of "Sunshine Air Express".

On the 14th April Spartan Airlines moved their London terminus from Croydon to Heston, thus putting them in direct competition with PSIOWA. The latter company commenced the route the following day but using a Courier which was faster than the Spartan Cruiser flight time being thirty minutes against forty for the latter. With the acquisition of the Envoy the route was strengthened with two services per day on Mondays, Tuesdays, Wednesdays and Thursdays with three on Fridays, five on Saturdays and four on Sundays. In order to cater for weekenders a Saturday lunchtime service was inaugurated which enabled passengers to stay in their offices until 12.30 (*Saturday morning working was normal in those days*) and still be on the Island by 14.00. By prior arrangement lunch baskets were provided on this service at a cost of 2/6 (*13p*). Weekenders naturally

wished to stay on the Island as long as possible and to cater for this a late service was provided leaving the Island at 20.25 on Sundays and Bank Holidays. On weekdays only the 08.40 from Shanklin and the 19.00 departure from Heston connected with the North Eastern Airways service from and to Leeds and Newcastle.

The south east London area contained a large population and in an endeavour to capture a slice of this market (Heston was to the west) PSIOWA negotiated an agreement with Cobham Air Routes and Provincial Airways, both of which were Croydon based. Passengers would begin their flight at Croydon on one of the above airlines and change to a PSIOWA flight at Portsmouth for their onward journey to Ryde or Shanklin. Cobham Air Routes Ltd was incorporated on May 3rd 1935 with a nominal capital of £30,000, the only directors being Sir Alan and Lady Cobham. Sir Alan was one of the outstanding pioneering airmen of the 20s and carried out trailblazing flights to Australia, the Cape of Good Hope and various journeys in and around Africa. He was well known for his National Air Day campaign and was instrumental in encouraging air mindedness. He originated and developed in-flight refuelling techniques and his company " Flight Refuelling Ltd" is still in existence today. His service departed Croydon at 09.00 and 14.45 with the flight time to Portsmouth being 25 minutes, the service carrying on to Bournemouth and Guernsey. The return flights departed Portsmouth for Croydon at 13.50 and 19.20 respectively. By this arrangement Isle of Wight residents had the choice of two routes to Guernsey, namely by PSIOWA to Southampton and then by Guernsey Airways or PSIOWA to Bournemouth and transferring to Cobham Air Services. Bookings for all these services could be made at PSIOWA's offices at 61, Union Street, Ryde. On the 3rd May Cobham

PSIOWA Airspeed Courier G-ABXL over Ryde.

Air Services suffered a fatal accident when Wessex G-ADEW ditched off the Needles with the loss of the pilot, Captain W. Ogden. It was first thought that the only passenger, a Mr C.F. Grainger, was also a casualty, but by the following day when all hope had faded he came ashore in a dinghy at Fowey, having been picked up by the S.S. Stanmore which was not equipped with radio. He later joined his wife and children at their holiday cottage in Seaview. Doubts were raised concerning the use of the Wessex on over water routes and this, plus problems with the landing ground in Guernsey, caused Sir Alan to sell his company, the buyer being Gordon Olley.

On the 7th May, which was the first day of issue of the King's Jubilee stamps an Airspeed Courier G-ACZL flown by Flying Officer WJ Scott made what is believed to be the first "official" air mail from Portsmouth to Shanklin. The twenty special letters were embossed by PSIOWA stamp and addressed to various persons in Portsmouth. On arrival at Shanklin they were posted and all were signed WJ Scott, Pilot.

According to a report in "The Portsmouth Evening News" on the 28th June the Envoy flew from Ryde to Heston in 17½ minutes, giving a ground speed of 210 mph. If the report was accurate and the aircraft was flying at normal cruising speed, then the tailwind component must have been in the order of 60 mph.

The Southern Railway was incensed by the low fares offered by PSIOWA as it was having an adverse effect on their partly subsidised partner, Spartan Airlines. The Railway wrote to all travel agents stating that if they dealt with

PSIOWA they would be banned from transacting business with the four railways, their shipping interests and Railway Air Services. This had a negative effect on PSIOWA but they were in a very weak bargaining position. the Southern insisted that the only way the ban could be lifted was if PSIOWA ceased operating the Heston-Island route and an undertaking not to re-introduce such a service in the future. PSIOWA had no option but to agree to these terms and the London route ceased operating at the end of the 1935 summer season.

From 22nd July a Southampton - Portsmouth - Paris service was started on a once daily *(not Sundays)* basis in each direction. It was advertised as a flight time of 90 minutes in a 175 mph airliner. The flight departed Southampton at 11.35, arriving at Portsmouth 15 minutes later. The Envoy left Portsmouth at noon and arrived at Le Bourget at 13.30 *(14.30 local time)*. The return service departed at 16.00 local time, arriving Portsmouth at 16.35 and Southampton 15 minutes later. The baggage allowance was 33lbs with 3d per lb excess.

The fares were:-

Single	£4.15.0 *(£4.75)*
15 day return	£7.15.0 *(£7.75)*
60 day return	£8.10.0 *(£8.50)*

There was also a special weekend return of £6.15.0 *(£6.75)*. The service could not have been a success as it ceased at the end of the season.

In 1935 the writer H.G. Wells contacted his friend, the poet Alfred Noyes, who lived at St Lawrence, near Ventnor, stating that he was looking for a house in which to die and would Noyes sell him his London house. Alfred Noyes invited Wells to the Island to discuss the matter and the latter flew to Shanklin where upon arrival he discovered that his baggage was missing. H.G. Wells was a supreme self-publicist and stated that the manuscript of "The Shape of Things to Come" was in his suitcase and that it represented a years work and was the only copy. He took the opportunity of creating nationwide publicity by writing to the Associated Press, Lord Beaverbrook and Scotland Yard, but his scheme was thwarted when he received a telephone call from a director of PSIOWA stating that his suitcase was in Newcastle. When the airline opened the case they found it only contained a pair of pyjamas and a change of underwear!

Children up to three years of age and not occupying a separate seat were carried at 10% of the adult fare, children 3 - 12 years of age at 50% of the adult fare except on the Ryde ferry when the fares were 3/- *(15p)* single and 5/- *(25p)* return. Dogs were also accepted on this route at 1/6 *(8p)* and 2/6 *(13p)*.

The baggage allowance was 33lbs with the usual restriction of 200lbs maximum for passengers plus luggage. The cost of excess baggage was 2d per pound but passengers travelling as a group were allowed to pool their allowance.

- LMJ Balfour's Puss Moth G-ABIY crashed on landing on 25th March.
- The Fox Moth G-ACCA was sold in June and was exported to Australia as VH-UTY.
- The total number of passengers carried during 1935 was approximately 42,000.

1936

After several years of what was undoubtably very rapid expansion, the time had come to consider PSIOWA's next moves. If further expansion was to be the aim then the company's capital base would have to be considerably increased and this would have probably meant bringing in an institutional shareholder with the inevitable loss of control by the directors. To avoid duplication and competition an agreement was reached with Railway Air Services and Channel Air Ferries that the Shoreham - Ryde route would be no longer be operated by PSIOWA and that the latter company would concentrate on its more profitable routes. The Heston - Island route, at the insistence of the Southern Railway, was dropped and never to be revived, the Shanklin extension of the Portsmouth - Ryde ferry cancelled and was not to be re-instated until 1938 and then to the new airport at Sandown (Iea). The remaining "hard core" routes were:- Portsmouth - Ryde ferry, Southampton - Ryde, Southampton - Ryde - Cowes, Ryde - Bournemouth.

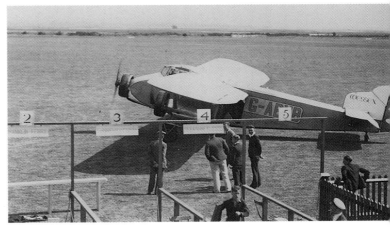

Wessex G-ABVB at Portsmouth   Credit: Chris Balfour

Monospar ST-25 Jubilee operated by PSIOWA from December 1936   Credit: Air Britain

ROUTE SUMMARY FROM 7th JUNE

		Journey time *(total not flight-time)*
Portsmouth - Ryde	Every 30 minutes	10 mins
Portsmouth - Shanklin	Eight times daily	20 mins
Portsmouth - Ryde - Bournemouth	Five times daily	40 mins
Southampton - Ryde - Shanklin	Five times daily	30 mins
Shoreham - Bournemouth		50 mins
Ryde - Bournemouth-Bristol-Cardiff	Twice daily	1 hr 10 mins-Bristol
		1 hr 45 mins-Cardiff
Ryde-Shanklin-Bournemouth	Five times daily	25 mins
Heston-Ryde-Shanklin	Various	30 mins-Ryde
		40 mins-Shanklin

SUMMARY OF FARES

	single		return		day return	
Portsmouth-Ryde	4/6	*(23p)*	8/6	*(43p)*	7/-	*(35p)*
Portsmouth-Shanklin	6/6	*(33p)*	12/6	*(63p)*	11/6	*(58p)*
Ryde-Bournemouth	11/6	*(55p)*	20/6	*(£1.03p)*	19/6	*(98p)*
Southampton-Ryde	7/-	*(35p)*	13/6	*(68p)*	12/6	*(63p)*
Southampton-Shanklin	9/-	*(45p)*	17/6	*(88p)*	16/6	*(83p)*
Shoreham-Bournemouth	25/6	*(£1.28p)*	47/-	*(£2.35p)*	44/6	*(£2.23p)*
Ryde-Bristol	30/6	*(£1.53p)*	58/-	*(£2.90p)*	49/-	*(£2.45p)*
Ryde-Cardiff	40/-	*(£2.00p)*	75/6	*(£3.78p)*	58/6	*(£2.93p)*

The frequencies of the services were:-
Portsmouth - Ryde ferry Operated skeleton services and on demand throughout the winter of 1935/36 with increased services during the spring and then during the peak seasons departures which were every twenty minutes to sunset.

Southampton - Ryde	Four times daily
Southampton - Cowes	Four times daily
Ryde - Bournemouth	Seven times daily

Unlike the Portsmouth - Ryde ferry all the above routes closed for the winter at the end of September *(Bournemouth on the 25th September)*.

To come into line with the long established Southern Railway Shipping practice, concessionary fares were introduced for the Island residents but only from Ryde.

Ryde - Portsmouth

Concessionary fare for Island residents	3/6 *(18p)* single 6/- *(30p)* return
Normal fare	4/6 *(23p)* single *(43p)* return

Ryde - Bournemouth

Concessionary fare for Island residents	9/- *(45p)* single 16/6 *(83p)* return
Normal fare	11/- *(55p)* single 20/6 *(£1.03p)* return

This concession was not available in the Ryde - Southampton route as this may well have invoked retaliatory action by Railway Air Services who also operated this sector as part of their Birmingham - Shoreham service.
PSIOWA also advertised in the Isle of Wight County Press that passengers holding the return halves of ordinary monthly or weekend rail and/or steamer tickets to Bournemouth, Southampton and Portsmouth may return by air by paying a supplement. The transfer could be conducted only at principal railway stations on the Island, but later extended to every station.
Two aircraft were sold in February, namely the Dragon G-ACRF to Australia and the Cobham Wessex G-ABAJ to Trafalgar Advertising Ltd, who fitted neon light tubes underneath the wings which were so arranged to spell the word "Oxo". The intention was to fly over London at night but whether this venture was successful is open to doubt as there were apparently insurmountable problems with the specially adapted aircraft electrics. In addition to the Wessex G-ABAJ several other changes to the fleet occurred in 1936.

On the 30th May the veteran Wessex G-ABVB, crashed at Ryde in full view of a number of spectators by hitting a hedge and ripping off the undercarriage. The pilot Mr R. Phillips was cut about the face but the five passengers were uninjured. The aircraft was written off but the demise of the Wessex caused unwanted capacity problems particularly as

this occurred at the start of the season.

With the Heston - Island and the Portsmouth - Paris routes discontinued the Envoy G-ADCA became surplus to requirements and was sold to Spain in August. On the 20th August three Couriers at Portsmouth and the Envoy at Heston were awaiting delivery to Spain but the Government introduced a non intervention policy and these aircraft were grounded. PSIOWA's Envoy managed to escape the net being flown to Paris by Captain Rollason of Rollason Aircraft Services. He promptly sold it to the office Générale de l'air in Paris who were acting as agents for the Spanish. A Spanish source *(Miranda and Mercado, Aviones en la Guerra Civil Espanõla Vol II)* stated that the Envoy arrived at El Prat, near Barcelona on or about the 22nd August. It was immediately sent to the front at Aragon and used as an improvised bomber and was likely to have been one of the aircraft that bombed Huesca on the 24th. On the 28th it was written off in a crash in France, presumably on a liaison flight. In the same month an additional Airspeed Courier was acquired. This aircraft was previously used by the manufacturers and was available for charter from time to time, its first C of A being 21st November 1933 and its registration was G-ACLR.

To replace the Wessex PSIOWA needed an economical twin engine aircraft but it was not until December 1936 that this became reality when they obtained two General Aircraft Monospar ST25 Jubilees. These aircraft had been originally operated by Crilly Airways Ltd, but were declared redundant when Crilly was taken over by British Airways. Their registrations were G-ADPK and G-ADPL. the ST25 had a cruising speed of 130mph which was 15mph faster than the ST-4 and unusually for those days the selling price included all instruments and a radio receiver equipped with D/F *(Direction Finding)*. This was in contrast with other manufacturers who regarded such items as "optional extras" and added them to the basic price.

During the winter of 1936/37 these two aircraft worked the Ryde ferry but in the summer of 1937 they also worked other routes as required. Pleasure flying remained popular, both at Portsmouth and Shanklin, with the prices depending upon duration and ranged from 4/6 *(23p)* to 10/- *(50p)*. Various charters were undertaken plus the scheduled service from Ryde to Goodwood during the race meetings. The Round the Island sightseeing tour from Portsmouth, Ryde and Shanklin continued and showed no loss of popularity.

The Portsmouth - Ryde ferry continued to increase with a total of 25,649 passengers carried on this route. In the hope that traffic could be sustained at somewhere near this level another aircraft was added to the fleet, the aircraft in question was the Prototype Monospar ST-10 G-ACTS and

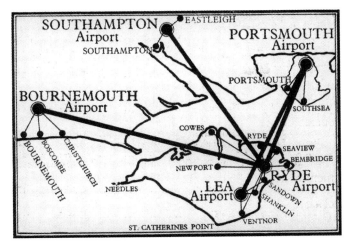

was delivered in November. When flown by H.M. Schofield it won the 1934 King's Cup Air Race at 134.16mph and by coincidence another future PSIOWA aircraft, the Napier engined Courier G-ACNZ flown by A.V.M. Borton, achieved a speed of 166mph before being disqualified.

The original low powered radio which served Portsmouth since 1934 was replaced by a higher powered permanent installation. The Ryde - Southampton service finished for the winter on 30th September and the Bournemouth route on the 25th of the same month.

During 1937 the Government at long last awoke to the threat from Nazi Germany and started the process of re-armament. The rolling "No war for ten years" rule was scrapped and the successive RAF expansion schemes implemented. This was to bring extra business to PSIOWA.

1937

It was always the intention of PSIOWA to develop Ryde into the major airport for the Isle of Wight and in 1934 they decided to equip the airport with modern facilities. New buildings were erected which included a control tower, a check in area, licensed restaurant and a waiting room. The complex was designed by a Ventnor architect in collaboration with F.L. Luxmoore and was built by the well known Norwich firm of structural engineers and aircraft manufacturers Boulton Paul Ltd. PSIOWA's confidence was well founded as it was used not only by their own services but as a scheduled stop on the Railway Air Service route from Shoreham to Birmingham. By 1937 a number of charters were using Ryde plus considerable numbers of private aircraft and in terms of movements Ryde equalled Portsmouth as the principal airport in the south. In view of this PSIOWA decided to form a specialist airport management company and with an eye to further business named it Vectis Airports Ltd, Vectis being the old Roman name for the Isle of Wight.

The Portsmouth - Ryde ferry was now an all year round operation and a regular but much reduced schedule was operated in winter. With the run up to the season services were gradually increased up to the maximum of every twenty minutes.

1937 was the best year of the 1930's for the internal airlines and PSIOWA was no exception with the Ryde ferry carrying 33,309 passengers, an increase of nearly 30% over 1936. At peak weekends additional services were run to clear the back log of passengers which at times were queueing at Ryde and Portsmouth.

1938

The Ryde ferry frequencies gradually built up as usual to its usual summer schedule of 25 flights per day in each direction.

During the spring the Ryde - Southampton service operated at three times daily but from 23rd May the summer service came into effect and the frequencies were increased to seven times daily including Sundays. The fares now were 7/9 *(38p)* single, return 15/- *(75p)* and day return 14/- *(70p)* which was inclusive of ground transport from Southampton Central Station and between Ryde airport to Sandown and Shanklin.

A new service commenced on 7th July from Portsmouth to Sandown *(Lea)* and operated twice daily in each direction including Sundays. The fares 8/- *(40p)* single, 15/- *(75p)* return. A day return was available at 12/6 (58p). The pick-up and set down points by company car were Portsmouth and Southsea Station, Shanklin Five Ways and at Sandown the Ocean Hotel.

In 1938 Railway Air Services started a Bournemouth - Ryde - Shoreham service and in order to avoid wasteful competition a formula of revenue sharing was agreed between Railway Air Services and PSIOWA, the latter company reducing its free baggage allowance to the 25lbs allowed by Railway Air Services. The through flights Bournemouth to Shoreham via Ryde were operated by Railway Air Services twice daily including Sundays and the other two flights which terminated at Ryde for connection to Portsmouth were flown by PSIOWA.

The timings from Bournemouth were:
To Shoreham (via Ryde)
RAS   10.35 and 17.35
To Ryde   PSIOWA 12.50 and 19.30

Tickets were interchangeable between the two companies, the fares being:

Portsmouth Aerocar

Credit: Portsmouth Aviation Ltd

Portsmouth Aerocar

Credit: Portsmouth Aviation Ltd

Bournemouth-Shoreham

Single	Return
Day Return	
22/- (£1.10)	41/6 (£2.08)
32/6 (£1.63)	

Bournemouth-Ryde

Single	Return
Day Return	
9/- (45p)	17/6 (88p)
15/- (75p)	

Credit: Chris Balfour

Free surface transport was provided and Shoreham passengers were entitled to travel First Class by train from and to the airport to Brighton, Hove and Worthing. Air passengers who wished to return by steamer/rail could apply at any railway station on the Island (or at Portsmouth Harbour Station), the tickets being converted to First Class sea/rail travel. The Railway Air Services de Havilland Dragon G-ADDI "City of Cardiff" was used on this route, its name being changed to "Island Maid". By now PSIOWA were fully licensed to carry out major overhauls and this aircraft was overhauled by them in the winter of 1936/37. Although owned by Railway Air Services it was from time to time operated by PSIOWA on the routes common to both companies.

Ryde Airport owned by PSIOWA. F.L. Luxmoore on right.   Credit: Chris Balfour

With re-armament in progress Lord Inskip was appointed Minister for co-ordination of Defence which entailed being a referee between the three service departments, an unenviable task! It was decided that Army anti aircraft gunners were in need of practice in tracking of aircraft, the flying part of which was contracted out to certain airlines, one of which was PSIOWA. Due to the Admiralty prohibited area around Portsmouth Dockyard from which civil aircraft were not allowed to overfly, these anti aircraft exercises had to be operated from Southampton (Eastleigh) which also had night flying facilities, PSIOWA using Couriers by day and Monospars by night. The Navy were offered the same facilities but refused as they had supreme confidence in their wonder weapon, the Multiple Pom Pom. On the rare occasions when they carried out such exercises it was always with a service aircraft which was normally a radio controlled, pilotless Queen Bee which could only fly straight and level! There is a well known tale, which it is believed originated in the RAF, that from the bridge of a warship in

mid channel the Admiral turned to his Gunnery Officer and said "Very strange, Commander, but we don't seem to be able to hit that aircraft". The Commander put his glass to his eye and replied "Yes Sir, but I think its a good thing, as we seem to have been firing at the Jersey Airways machine for the last five minutes".

The anti aircraft contract involved some very intensive flying, one of the pilots being the famous record breaking Amy Johnson who was to meet her death in an Airspeed Oxford over the Thames estuary in January 1941.

From commencing scheduled services in 1932 to December 1938 PSIOWA carried over 200,000 passengers without injury.

During the summer of 1938 the Southampton - Ryde service

1939

The services in 1939 were:-

Portsmouth - Ryde ....1st Jan - 22nd Jan ....Five times daily
Portsmouth - Ryde ....23rd Jan - 25th Feb ....Six times daily
Portsmouth - Ryde ....26th Feb - 31st March.....Seven times daily
Portsmouth - Ryde ....1st April - 15th April.......Six times daily
Portsmouth - Ryde ....16th April - 13th May ....Seven times daily *(not Sundays)*
Portsmouth - Ryde ....14th May - 30th June......Eleven times daily
Portsmouth - Ryde ....1st July - 22nd July ....Twelve times daily
Portsmouth - Ryde ....23rd July to start of War .Twenty times daily
....*(extra services according to demand)*
Southampton - Ryde ....Until 2nd April ....Twice daily on weekdays
Southampton - Ryde ....3rd April - 30th April......Twice daily inc Sundays
Southampton - Ryde ....1st May - September ....Thrice daily inc Sundays

Ryde - Bournemouth ....3rd April - 25th May.......Twice daily inc Sundays
Ryde - Bournemouth ....26th May - 16th July.......Four times daily inc Sundays
Ryde - Bournemouth ....17th July - September......Six times daily inc Sundays
Portsmouth - Sandown (Lea)..From 7th July ....Twice daily

The 11.35 ex Southampton was flown by Great Western and Southern Airlines and was a through flight via Ryde to Shoreham. G.W. & S.A. was, in the south, the successor to R.A.S. and the route was worked on a revenue sharing basis.

Surface transport between town centres and the airport was included with the exception of Portsmouth when transport by company car was provided for the sum of 9d (4p).

For the first time the day return applied without restriction of time, but, in addition, an excursion was offered from the Isle of Wight only up to 13.00 and returning after 17.30 at 6/- (30p).

On the Isle of Wight taxi fares were advertised for passengers who wished to travel by taxi instead of by Southern Vectis buses. Example fares from Ryde Airport were:

Fares	Single	Return	Day Return
Portsmouth - Ryde	5/- (25P)	9/6 (48p)	8/6 (43p)
Southampton - Ryde	5/- (25P)	9/6 (48p)	8/6 (43p)
Ryde - Bournemouth	9/- (45P)	17/6 (88p)	15/- (75p)

Seaview 4/- (20p)		Newport.................10/- (50p)	
Bembridge..............6/- (30p)		East Cowes.............12/- (60p)	
Sandown.................6/- (30p)		Ventnor 15/- (75p)	
Shanklin 10/- (50p)			

had built up satisfactorily with just under 4,000 passengers being carried during this period, and encouraged by this PSIOWA decided to operate a winter service from 1st October at a frequency of twice daily including Sundays.

Despite Neville Chamberlain's post Munich speech of "Peace in our Time" in September 1938, the general public perceived that war was inevitable which resulted in a lesser number of people travelling for pleasure, resulting in the figures for the Ryde ferry being only 27,704 *(1937 - 33,309).*

The Air Navigation Act of 1936 dictated that as from the 1st November 1938 an airline had to be in possession of a licence issued by the Air Transport Licencing Authority and which stipulated the routes to be worked by an individual airline. To operate without such a licence would be to

commit an offense but in practice the airlines were given a few weeks grace.

The licences awarded to PSIOWA were:
Portsmouth - Ryde - Bournemouth
Bournemouth -Ryde
Portsmouth - Sandown
Southampton - Ryde

The 45 minute "Round the Island" sightseeing flight continued in 1939, the fare being 19/6 *(97½p)* which is in stark contrast to the cost in 1932 of the 60 minute flight at 38/6 *(£1.93).* There was another excursion consisting of a flight from Portsmouth to Ryde and then a coach trip round the Island before returning to Ryde for the flight back to Portsmouth. The cost of this was 14/6 *(73p).*

To fulfil the demands of the anti aircraft contract two more Couriers were added to the fleet, G-ACLF in April and, after the commencement of hostilities, the Napier engine Courier G-ACNZ, which was refitted with a Lynx engine. Two aircraft were acquired in October 1939, namely Miles M3 Falcon Major G-ADHI and Miles Falcon Six G-AECC but both were impressed in March 1940.

In June 1939 the ex Sir Alan Cobham joy rider Airspeed Ferry G-ABSI was acquired but in view of its condition it needed a complete overhaul, this being carried out by the late William H. Llewellyn, author of "Pigs and wings and other things". He states that it was put into service on the Ryde Ferry but after flying in Couriers it must have been a bit of a shock to passengers. He also, on behalf of the company, obtained from a scrap merchant an Avro Tutor (*ex K3237*). Although this wreck was in pieces it would appear that everything was in good condition and therefore it was rebuilt by Llewellyn; fitted with a spare Armstrong Siddeley Lynx IVc and put to work on the anti aircraft contract as G-AFZW.

When the above Airspeed ferry was operated by Cobham's Air Circus, Sir Alan came up against an Air Ministry regulation which stated that an aircraft that was fitted to carry ten passengers must be equipped with radio. He protested that with passengers aboard he would always be in sight of the airfield and therefore when applied to joy-riding, the regulation was nonsense. Nevertheless the bureaucrats were adamant and in face of this Sir Alan had no option but to undertake to fit radio in place of one passenger seat, thus only being able to carry nine passengers. Bureaucracy was unabashed and informed Sir Alan that as he could only carry nine passengers he would not require a radio! Eventually commonsense prevailed and a special dispensation was granted.

On the 3rd September the Air Navigation (*Restriction in Time of War*) Order 1939 was promulgated and all commercial flying to the Island ceased.

At the start of the War PSIOWA continued with its now intensified anti aircraft contract, but due to the perceived vulnerability of Portsmouth to air attack they operated from Cardiff with up to twelve aircraft per night. The above perception in proved to be correct as in July 1940 Airspeed suffered the dubious distinction of being the first aircraft factory of the war to be hit. At some date during the war PSIOWA returned to Portsmouth and were heavily engaged as a repair organisation with over 5,000 damaged aircraft, mainly Oxfords, passing through their hands. On the 8th February 1943 the company changed it's name to the much simplified "Portsmouth Aviation Ltd".

During their pre-war operations PSIOWA, along with other independent operators, were always short of cash and it would not be unreasonable to argue that it was the profits from the anti aircraft contract that put the company on a sounder financial footing. In 1939 they were the only surviving independent airline in the South of England and it was only the hard work and single mindedness of Balfour and Luxmoore that kept the company afloat.

During the War Railway Air Services and PSIOWA had a series of discussions, the purpose of which was to plan their post-war activities. Agreement was finally reached on the 9th March 1945 whereby the Southern Railway would lend Portsmouth Aviation Ltd the necessary share capital to take up shares; the restructured company requiring a capital of between £100,000 and £150,000. Portsmouth Aviation would then operate as Isle of Wight Airways Ltd, a name they first registered in the early 1930's but had remained dormant. They planned to form a holding company to be called Aviation and General Trust Ltd but the name was not available and they therefore settled for Aviation and Industrial Trust Ltd. It would appear that Railway Air Services would operate the longer routes while Isle of Wight Airways Ltd would concentrate on the following:-

Isle of Wight - Shoreham
Isle of Wight - Portsmouth
Isle of Wight - Southampton
Isle of Wight - Bournemouth

In theory, except for through flights, Railway Air Services would not have traffic rights over the above routes but were allowed rights to fill vacant seats! Railway Air Services insisted that Isle of Wight Airways staff would have pay and superannuation schemes based on railway practice, and this, combined with other factors would have meant, that over a period of time, Isle of Wight Airways would have been swallowed whole by the railways. This, of course never happened as the Labour Government nationalised all air transport.

Immediately after the War the company was engaged in charter work using de Havilland Dragon Rapides, Airspeed Consuls and Percival Proctors, but this ceased in 1947.

They also entered the field of aircraft design and manufacture and produced a light transport aircraft named the "Portsmouth Aerocar". Drawing on their very considerable experience on short haul high frequency services it was decided that the twin boom, high wing configuration was the best solution for quick turn rounds and passenger access. six models were to be retained by the

Airspeed ferry G-ABSI at Portsmouth.

Credit: Shoreham Airport Collection

Ex Sir Alan Cobham Airspeed ferry operated by PSIOWA in 1939.

Credit: Shoreham Airport Collection

company for their proposed re-introduction of their scheduled services. Two versions were proposed but the only one actually built was fitted with the more powerful 155hp Cirrus Major engines. It was apparently a viceless aircraft which offered low operating costs and a number of orders were received. Unfortunately during this period there was a shortage of raw materials added to which the Government instituted a severe credit squeeze which affected most industries. It was these factors that prevented production which was unfortunate as early indications were that a good market existed.

Since that time Portsmouth Aviation Ltd has concentrated on technical activities, being an approved design organisation for the CAA and MOD, carrying out research and development studies for the above including the design of various components and airborne ordnance.

At the time of writing the company remains a family owned business, which if not unique, must be very rare in the aviation business.

Aircraft of PSIOWA & their Fates

AVRO 504K G-AAFE Certificate of Airworthiness 31st May 1929. Used for Joy Riding and instruction at Shanklin (Apse). Withdrawn from use in December 1930.

AVRO 504K G-AAFT
Ex RAF J8379, Certificate of Airworthiness 26th March 1929 and pending the incorporation of Inland Flying Services Ltd, was registered in the name of AB Forsyth. Used at Shanklin (Apse) for Joy Riding and instruction but withdrawn from use in March 1931.

de Havilland 60X Moth G-AAAG (C/N 697) Certificate of Airworthiness 22nd August 1928. On the 7th November 1934 it was flying over the Solent in adverse weather conditions, later called IFR and spun into the sea killing both occupants. It is likely that the amateur pilot became disorientated in cloud and was too low to effect a recovery. Although the Moth was still registered in the name of PSIOWA it was actually operated by Portsmouth Aero Club and therefore no direct blame could be attached to PSIOWA.

de Havilland Puss Moth G-ABIY (C/N 2134) Certificate of Airworthiness 28th February 1931. Property of LMJ Balfour who flew it in the 1931 King's Cup Air Race coming in fourth. It remained in the ownership of Mr Balfour but used by PSIOWA. It crashed and was written off in March 1935.

de Havilland 60 Gipsy Moth G-ABJH (C/N 1838) Certificate of Airworthiness 14th April 1931. Property of LMJ Balfour but transferred to PSIOWA in January 1933. Impressed into RAF in December 1939 as X5111.

Klemm L.27 III G-ABJX (C/N 247) Certificate of Airworthiness 27th March 1931. Like the Spartan Three Seater this aircraft was equipped to carry two passengers in the front cockpit thus making this a very economical Joy Riding aircraft. Used at both Shanklin and Portsmouth but mainly at the latter. The Klemm was a German aircraft but powered by a 95hp Cirrus III engine. Scrapped 1946.

Spartan three seater G-ABLJ (C/N 59) Delivered 22nd July 1932. Sold to Yapton Aero Club in September 1938. Sold to various private owners and passed to A.T.C. in 1943.

Westland Wessex G-ABVB (W.A 2156)
Delivered 6th May 1932. Crashed at Ryde 30th May 1936. Pilot slightly injured.
Passengers unscathed.

Westland Wessex G-ABAJ (W.A1897)
Ex Sabena. Returned to UK March 1935 and used on Ryde ferry. Sold February 1936 to Trafalgar Advertising Ltd, scrapped 1938.

de Havilland Fox Moth G-ACIG (C/N 4072)
Delivered 12th July 1933. Impressed into RAF as instructional airframe with Hampstead ATC.
Broken up 1946.

de Havilland Fox Moth G-ACCA (C/N 4041)
Delivered September 1932. Sold to Australia as VH-UTY in June 1935.

de Havilland Dragon (6077) G-ACRF
Delivered on the 18th May 1934. Sold to Australia 1936. Crashed at Archerfield 19th April 1954.

Airspeed Courier G-ACZL (C/N 25)

Delivered April 1935. Impressed into the RAF in March 1940. Damaged beyond repair on take off from Shenfield, Essex on 15th October 1940.

Airspeed Courier G-ADAX (C/N 26)
Delivered April 1935. Impressed for use by No 3 ferry pool A.T.A., an abbreviation for the Air Transport Auxiliary, an organisation of civilian pilots which during the Second World War delivered aircraft of all types from the factory to the Armed Services. Small civil aircraft such as the Courier were used as taxis for delivery and pick up of pilots. On the 17th March 1941 it was flown to Portsmouth for scrapping.

Airspeed Courier G-ADAY (C/N 27)
Delivered April 1935. Impressed as G-ADAX above and scrapped Portsmouth March 1941.

Airspeed Courier G-ACLF (C/N 12)
Ex North Eastern Airways. Delivered April 1939. Impressed March 1940. Scrapped Kemble 1943.
Airspeed Courier G-ACLR (C/N 11)
Ex Airspeed. Delivered to Portsmouth, Southsea and Isle of Wight Aviation Ltd August 1936. Impressed March 1940. Crashed Bolt Head, Devon on the !st August 1942.

General Aircraft Monospar ST-4 G-ABVN (C/N 2) Delivered 19th August 1932. Sold to private individual in December 1933. From 1939 no information as to the fate of this was known, but the fuselage turned up in 1954 at Bankstown Airport, Sydney, New South Wales. How it came to be there is a mystery.

Centre of PSIOWA timetable 1939

Cover of PSIOWA timetable 1939

General Aircraft Monospar ST-25 G-ADPK Jubilee (C/N 55) Ex Crilly Airways. Delivered December 1936. Impressed March 1940 and scrapped in August 1942.

General Aircraft Monospar ST-25 G-ADPL Jubilee (C/N 56) Ex Crilly Airways. Delivered December 1936. Impressed March 1940, fate unknown.

General Aircraft Monospar ST-10 G-ACTS (C/N 32) Ex General Aircraft Ltd, delivered November 1937. Impressed April 1940, used by the Royal Navy in 1943. Fate not known.

Airspeed Courier G-ACNZ (C/N 20)
This aircraft was originally supplied to D Napier and Sons Ltd to flight test their new Napier Rapier IV 16 cylinder "H" engine of 350hp, the power being absorbed by a four bladed propeller. Although owned by Napier's it was registered in the name of Air Vice Marshal A.G. Borton, a director, who flew it in the 1934 King's Cup Air Race at an average speed of 166mph before being eliminated. There were considerable problems with overheating with this engine, particularly after prolonged taxiing and to overcome this the recommended procedure was to shut down for fifteen minutes, switch on and take off as quickly as possible before the problem re-occurred! PSIOWA acquired it in November 1939 and replaced the Rapier with a Lynx. Impressed March 1940 and scrapped at Kemble April 1944.0

Airspeed Envoy Series 1 G-ADCA (C/N 36)
Delivered May 1935. Sold to Spain in August 1936, see text for details of fate.

Airspeed Courier G-ABXN (C/N 7)
Although the records of this aircraft indicate that it was never owned by P.S.I.O.W.A. there is photographic evidence to show that at some period it was certainly operated by them. The most probable explanation is that it was chartered to P.S.I.O.W.A. to cover a peak period. This was the prototype and was the last aircraft assembled at York before Airspeed moved to Portsmouth. It was specially modified for Sir Alan Cobham for his attempt on a non stop flight to India. The aircraft was to be re-fuelled in mid-air from a Handley Page W.10 tanker, a hatch was incorporated in the roof so that the second pilot/navigator/hose operator could catch the hose and fill the fuselage overload tank. They were well into the flight when the throttle linkage failed, thus forcing a return to Malta when a wheels up landing was made. The aircraft was shipped back home and returned to Standard. It was scrapped he A.T.A. Ferry Pool, White Waltham in September 1940.

Airspeed Ferry G-ABSI (C/N 4)
Built for Sir Alan Cobham in April 1932. Subsequently CWA Scott and Air Publicity Ltd to Portsmouth, Southsea and Isle of Wight Aviation Ltd June 1939. Impressed into RAF and used by station flight, Halton until November 1940. Taken into store at 51MU before being given to 474 Squadron ATC Derbyshire.

PSIOWA Aircraft Specification

Airspeed Courier

Power Plant	One 240HP Armstrong Siddeley Lynx IVC
Wingspan	47' 0"
Length	28 '6"
Maximum all up weight	3,900lbs
Maximum speed	153 MPH
Cruising speed	132 MPH
Range	635 miles
Accommodation	1 crew + 5 passengers
Production	16

Airspeed Envoy

Power Plant	2 X 240HP Armstrong Siddeley Lynx IVC
Wingspan	52' 4"
Length	34 '6"
Maximum all up weight	5,850lbs
Maximum speed	174 MPH
Cruising speed	153 MPH
Range	650 miles
Accommodation	1 or 2 crew + 8 passengers
Production	61

Airspeed Ferry

Power Plant	3 X 130HP de Havilland Gipsy Majors
Wingspan	55' 0"
Length	39 '8"
Maximum all up weight	5,400lbs
Maximum speed	108 MPH
Cruising speed	90 MPH
Range	340 miles
Accommodation	Up to 10 passengers
Production	4

AVRO 504K

Power Plant	The 504K was fitted with a number of different power plants, the most popular being a 100hp Gnome, 110hp Le Rhone or a 130hp Clerget
Wingspan	36' 0"
Length	29 '5"
Maximum all up weight	1,829lbs
Maximum speed	95 MPH
Cruising speed	75 MPH
Range	250 miles
Accommodation	Normally two but often converted to three
Production	Not known - many thousands

de Havilland Dragon II

Power Plant	2 X 130HP de Havilland Gipsy Majors
Wingspan	47' 4"
Length	34 '6"
Maximum all up weight	4,500lbs
Maximum speed	134 MPH
Cruising speed	114 MPH
Range	545 miles
Accommodation	Pilot + up to 10 passengers
Production	115 + 87 in Australia

de Havilland 60X Moth

Power Plant	90hp Cirrus III
Wingspan	30' 0"
Length	23 '81/2"
Maximum all up weight	1,550lbs
Maximum speed	95 MPH
Cruising speed	85 MPH
Range	430 miles
Accommodation	2/3
Production	403 of this variant of Moth in UK, many additional aircraft built overseas

de Havilland Fox Moth

Power Plant	One 130HP de Havilland Gipsy Majors
Wingspan	30' 101/2"
Length	25 '9"
Maximum all up weight	2,070lbs
Maximum speed	113 MPH
Cruising speed	96 MPH
Range	360 miles
Accommodation	Pilot + 4 passengers
Production	98 + 2 in Australia and 54 in Canada

de Havilland Gipsy Moth

Power Plant	100hp Gipsy I
Wingspan	30' 0"
Length	29 '11"
Maximum all up weight	1,650lbs
Maximum speed	102 MPH
Cruising speed	85 MPH
Range	320 miles
Accommodation	2
Production	595 plus overseas production

General Aircraft Monospar ST-4

Power Plant	2 X 85HP Pobjoy R
Wingspan	40' 2"
Length	26 '4"
Maximum all up weight	2,550lbs
Maximum speed	130 MPH
Cruising speed	115 MPH
Range	540 miles
Accommodation	Pilot + 4 passengers

General Aircraft Monospar ST-10

Power Plant	2 X 90HP Pobjoy Niagara I
Wingspan	40' 2"
Length	26 '4"
Maximum all up weight	2,750lbs
Maximum speed	142 MPH
Cruising speed	130 MPH
Range	585 miles
Accommodation	4
Production	2

General Aircraft Monospar ST 25 Jubilee

Power Plant	2 X 90HP Pobjoy Niagara II
Wingspan	40' 2"
Length	26 '4"
Maximum all up weight	2,875lbs
Maximum speed	142 MPH
Cruising speed	130 MPH
Range	585 miles
Accommodation	Pilot + up to 5 passengers
Production	59

Klemm L.27A III

Power Plant	95HP Cirrus III
Wingspan	42' 71/2"
Length	24 '71/2"
Maximum all up weight	1,584lbs
Maximum speed	109 MPH
Cruising speed	Not known
Range	Not known
Accommodation	3
Production	Four of this model imported into UK

Spartan Three Seater

Power Plant	115hp Cirrus Hermes IIB
Wingspan	28' 10"
Length	26 '3"
Maximum all up weight	1,850lbs
Maximum speed	107 MPH
Cruising speed	95 MPH
Range	260 miles
Accommodation	3
Production	26

Westland Wessex

Power Plant	3 X 140HP Armstrong Siddeley Genet Majors IA
Wingspan	57' 6"
Length	38' 0"
Maximum all up weight	6,300lbs
Maximum speed	122 MPH
Cruising speed	108 MPH
Range	340 miles
Accommodation	2 crew + up to 8 passengers
Production	10

Spartan Aircraft Ltd & Spartan Airlines

Spartan 3-Seater G-ABAZ 'Island Queen' outside its 'hanger'
at Shanklin Landguard Manor

Credit: Tom Hiett

Between the wars a company named Whitehall Securities Corporation Ltd was very active in aviation investment and anybody who researches this period will frequently come across the name. It was part of the Pearson Group of companies which had substantial interest in newspapers, public contracting, oil etc; Whitehall Securities being set up to manage their aviation interests. All the shares in Pearsons were held by the Cowdray family *(Viscount Cowdray)* and his second son, The Hon. Clive Pearson managed the enterprise. By the end of 1933, they had majority holdings in a number of aviation enterprises including Saunders Roe (SARO) and Spartan.

Spartan Aircraft Ltd

While being employed as a draughtsman for Supermarine, a Mr O.E. Simmonds, later Sir Oliver, had the idea of building a two seater biplane with interchangeable wing panels and tailplane using symmetrical aerofoil sections, the motive being to provide an aircraft that was not only cheaper than the market leader, the de Havilland 60 Moth, but requiring

minimum maintenance and spares holdings. The interchangeability did not only apply to the wings but also other components such as both halves of the undercarriage, the tailplane and elevators. The fin and rudder were also designed to be swapped with the horizontal empennage and even the bracing wires were identical. The engine was to be a 95HP Cirrus III and the resultant aircraft was named the Simmonds Spartan. In March 1928 Simmonds resigned from Supermarine and with the help of a skilled woodworker, Mr Thomas Hiett, actually designed and built his first aircraft at his home at 65, Portsmouth Road, Woolston, Southampton. The fuselage was built in the lounge and the wings in the bedrooms but in order to get these components out of the house he had to remove all the frames from the front doors and windows. The aircraft, registered G-EBYU, was assembled at his new production centre at the Rolling Mills, Archers Road, Southampton and the first flight was conducted by Flight Lieutenant Webster of the R.A.F. High Speed Flight; who also raced it in the King's Cup Air Race on 20 - 21st July 1928 at 73.06mph. It was exhibited at the Berlin Aero Show in October, being flown by the C.F.I. of

Spartan Arrow G-AAWY in workshops at Cowes

Credit: Tom Hiett

the Purbeck Flying Club, H.W.R. Banting with Lt. Col. Strange as passenger. The outward flight time was seven hours and ten minutes while the homeward leg was achieved in five hours, fifty five minutes.

Simmonds Aircraft Ltd was then formed with a capital of £20,000 and through C.G.Grey, the editor of 'The Aeroplane' Simmonds was introduced to Lt. Colonel Louis Strange M.C. D.S.O. D.F.C., a First World War pilot, who underwent what was probably a unique experience in that trying to change a jammed drum on his Lewis gun he stood up in the cockpit, his Martinsyde went out of control, climbed and he was left hanging on to the jammed drum. After a lot of struggling, he managed to obtain a more secure hold by grabbing an interplane strut and was successful in hauling himself back into the cockpit. No parachutes were issued to the R.F.C. at that time and therefore if the drum had become free the result would have been fatal.

At the start of the Second World War in 1939 Louis Strange rejoined the R.A.F. and became the first Officer Commanding of the Airborne Forces Parachute Training School at Ringway and also the first Officer Commanding of the M.S.F.U. (Merchant Ship Fighter Unit). He left the service in 1945 as a Wing Commander. He died in 1966 at the age of 75.

Reverting to 1928, Lt Colonel Strange was very impressed with the low production costs and Simmonds' novel ideas and therefore agreed to join the company as test pilot and salesman. For flight testing purposes Simmonds rented a hanger at Hamble, the completed aircraft being towed from Woolston for testing either by Louis Strange or by one of his R.A.F. contacts stationed at Calshot. Between 1928 and 1930

some forty nine aircraft had been ordered, the majority being fitted with the 100hp Hermes I engine, although alternatives such as the 100hp Gipsy I, the 120hp Gipsy II or the 105hp Hermes II were offered. The largest single order was from National Flying Services who ordered twelve, although not all were delivered. The first production aircraft was bought by Philadelphia based Scott Aeronautic Company as NC512E and was flight tested by a Major J.S. Owens of the 28th Division who said it was "a great little ship".

Two individual aircraft are worth mentioning, the first being G-AAMI (C/N 35) which was sold to Wilhelm Omsted of Oslo in April 1930. It was registered as LN-ABG, fitted with skis and used on the Norwegian East Greenland Expedition where it completed over 45,000 miles of arctic flying. It was later acquired by the Norwegian Internal Airline Widerøe who operated it on schedules to remote places. Another Simmonds Spartan was ZK-ABU which was purchased by Air Travel *(PTY)* Ltd of New Zealand and achieved fame as being the first aircraft to land on the Waiko Gorge glacier. One local aircraft was G-AAHA *(C/N17)* which was bought by Charlie Coombs, of Shanklin Flying Services in June 1929 and operated out of Landguard Manor, Shanklin for two years. An amusing story is told by Tom Hiett in Air Britain Digest dated May-June 1977 about a William Andrews who was flying a Simmonds Spartan with a specially fitted variable pitch propeller. When one blade detached itself, the resulting vibration caused the engine to depart from the airframe, the aircraft to mush down and to be completely destroyed in the crash. Amazingly, Andrews was relatively unhurt, the only injury being a bump on the head, but he was not yet out of trouble as he was soaked in

'Island Queen' note later colour scheme - all red fuselage.

Credit: Tom Hiett

Spartan 3-Seater at Shanklin Apse, early 30's

Credit: John King

Spartan 3-Seater G-ABAZ 'Island Queen'.

Credit: Tom Hiett

petrol from the ruptured tank, the contents of which were dyed red. He was rushed to hospital where he was diagnosed as having scarlet fever and placed in isolation but escaped through a window and a telephone call to Hamble saved him from any more tribulations!

Three aircraft were modified by having the wingspan increased by four feet which gave an improved performance and a number of others converted to Three Seaters, of which three operated in the home market. One of these, G-AAHV *(C/N 44),* was bought by the Reverend C.D.C. Boulton who used it as an open air travelling pulpit. These Three Seaters should not be confused with the Spartan Three Seater which was a different aircraft.

 One of the original two seaters was experimentally fitted with a revolutionary engine named the Redrup Fury which was a seven cylinder swashplate engine with a frontal diameter of only 18 inches thus offering minimum drag. It was reputed to be able to run on margarine but the author has been unable to establish if it was in any way successful when running on this somewhat unconventional fuel. What is known, however, is that it was not particularly successful running on petrol! A total of twenty four aircraft were registered in Britain. Simmonds was also successful overseas, selling six to New Zealand, five to Australia and two to Canada. There is some discrepancy in the

constructors numbers and the author has heard from more than one source a persistent story that a number of aircraft, believed six, were loaded on a lighter and trans-shipped off Cowes for delivery to some unidentified clandestine Air Force. Despite its low maintenance costs, the Simmonds Spartan was handicapped by its initial cost which in 1930 was £700 for a Two Seater and £735 for the Three Seater, whereas the well established Gipsy Moth could be bought for £650. By late 1929 the company was experiencing severe financial difficulties and was facing possible liquidation but through the offices of Louis Strange, Simmonds met Captain Harold Balfour M.C. M.P. *(later Lord Balfour of Inchrye)* who was instrumental in persuading Whitehall Securities to take over the company. The company was completely reconstituted with a capital of £110,000 and the name changed to Spartan Aircraft Ltd with Whitehall Securities having a controlling interest. The Board appointed were Sir Alliot Verdon-Roe, Captain H.H. Balfour M.C., Lt Colonel L.A. Strange M.C. D.S.O. D.F.C., A.E. Chambers M.I.C.E., J. de C. Ballardie and W.D.L. Roberts. Simmonds then resigned and later started a company named Simmonds Aero Accessories which became well known for it's fibre inserted self locking nuts. This became a very successful company producing aero accessories in Britain, France, Poland, U.S.A., Canada and Australia and at its peak had up to 10,000 employees. In 1931 he became Unionist M.P. for

Spartan Arrow, Somerton 1936. Driver 'Wink' + one.   Credit: Millichap/Croydon Airport Society

Last surviving Spartan Arrow   Credit: Air Britain

Spartan Cruiser I G-ABTY
Credit: British Hovercraft Corporation

Birmingham (Duddeston) and remained in that office until he lost his seat in the 1945 election. He was knighted in 1944 for services to Industry but in 1948 disillusioned with post war Britain, he sold all his interests and moved to the Bahamas. He died in Guernsey on 26th July 1985 aged 88.

In the early 1930's almost everybody was suffering from the World-wide recession and as Whitehall Securities Ltd had a majority interest in the well known flying boat builders Saunders Roe Ltd, it was decided to move Spartan to Saunders works at East Cowes, Isle of Wight. Like most defence contractors, Saunders Roe were lacking in orders and therefore the move not only saved money but helped to retain the skilled workforce at Cowes.

Saunders Roe/Spartan acting upon information provided by operators that the symmetrical wing sections, while presenting no difficulties to experienced pilots, caused considerable problems for trainees. It was decided to undertake a re-design which consisted of a two foot increase in wingspan, an orthodox high lift Clark Y aerofoil, an improved fin and rudder of increased chord and roomier cockpits, the aircraft being named the Spartan Arrow and Spartan Three Seater.

The prototype Arrow G-AAWY was fitted with a Hermes II of 105hp but the first two production aircraft G-AAWZ and G-ABBE were powered by a 120hp Gipsy II. The prototype was sold to Shanklin Flying Services who replaced the Hermes II with a 120hp Gipsy II. It was later, as part of the business, sold to the Isle of Wight Flying Club who operated it up to the outbreak of War. During the War it was dismantled and various components were used to construct a

glider, details of which the author has been unable to ascertain. At least two survived the War, namely G-ABWP which was operated by the Shuttleworth Trust and ex G-ACHG which was still flying with the Östersunds Flygklubb in 1951. A total of twenty eight were built, the last six having ailerons only on the lower mainplanes. Of the Three Seaters, nineteen Mark I's were built followed by seven Mark II's. These latter aircraft differed from the Mark I by moving the pilot's cockpit to the front and fitting an inverted Hermes engine. These modifications not only improved the pilot's vision, but gave the passengers better access.

The best known Three Seater was the Mark I G-ABKK *(C/N 58)* operated by Pauline Gower and Dorothy Spicer in 1933 and named "Helen of Troy". In that year they visited 185 towns in support of the British Hospitals Air Pageants, but after they parted company with "Helen of Troy" it was written off in a take off collision at Coventry while being operated by Campbell Black's Air Circus. All the Mark II's, with the exception of the prototype G-ABTR, were powered by the 120hp Hermes IV, the prototype being fitted with a 115hp Hermes II and was the only one to have an enclosed cockpit fitted. It was operated by Spartan Airlines from 1933 to 1936 when it was sold. In 1947 it was one of a number of pre-war light aircraft that were deliberately burnt at Gatwick.

The next project for Spartan Aircraft was the Clipper which was a low wing monoplane of wood construction with seating for two side by side. To save costs and tooling, the outer wing panels were 'bought in' Monospar ST.4 wings which were readily available. Piloted by Louis Strange it first flew on the 14th December 1932 and after

Spartan Cruiser II   Credit: Croydon Airport Society

Spartan Cruiser II   Credit: Mike Hooks

modifications was registered G-ACEG. During tests at A.&A.E.E. in June 1933 it suffered wing flutter and was severely criticised, the official language being "Suffers serious wing oscillation in rectilinear flight at 100mph and was not fitted with any mass or aerodynamic balances". Modifications were recommended but despite the report a Certificate of Airworthiness was issued on the 29th of the same month. The Clipper was never retested and was retained by the manufacturer as a communications aircraft. With its 75hp Pobjoy R, it was underpowered and in 1938 was fitted with a 90hp Pobjoy Niagara; the aircraft remaining in service until it was destroyed in an air raid on Cowes in May 1942.

The Air Ministry issued a specification *(21/28)* for a mailplane which could fly a 1000 miles at 150MPH and carry 1000lbs of mail, the specification calling for the aircraft to have the ability to maintain level flight with one engine out of action. SARO *(Saunders Roe)* /Spartan in conjunction with Edgar Percival, the well known aircraft designer, set about designing and building such an aircraft as

a joint venture, but Percival subsequently pulled out and it was left to Saunders Roe to complete the project under the direction of H.E. *(Harry)* Broadsmith, who was brought in by Sir Alliot Verdon Roe as General Manager and Chief Designer. The aircraft was designated as the A.24 Mailplane and was of all wood construction, the power being provided by three 120hp Gipsy III engines. It was a low wing monoplane with fixed undercarriage with a single fin and rudder. In an attempt to improve stability it was later fitted with twin fins and rudders but the modification was not successful and it soon reverted to its original configuration. The first flight was from Cowes *(Somerton)* on the 1st June 1931, its pilot being Leslie Ash, Saunders Roe Chief Test Pilot. Before starting on a sales tour in 1932 it was fitted with small windows in the mail compartment but nevertheless accommodation was rather cramped. The mailplane was named "Blackpool" at that town's Stanley Park Aerodrome and on the 15th June it departed for Drigh Road, Karachi, where it arrived six days later. It was flown by Neville Stack with engineer Fred Taylor and accompanied by William Courteney, Air Correspondent of

Spartan Cruiser II G-ACDX at Portsmouth

Credit: Chris Balfour

Spartan Cruiser II G-ACDX landing at Croydon

Credit: Croydon Airport Society

Spartan Cruisers at Bembridge

Credit: Henry Nobbs

FLEET LIST FOR 1933	
Cruiser I	G-ABTY from April
Cruiser II	G-ACDW "Faithful City" from May
Cruiser II	G-ACDX "Hampshire" from June
3 Seater	G-ABTR from April - joy-riding and Air Taxi work

the London Evening Standard. Demonstrations were given to the Director of Civil Aviation and upon completion of these the journey home was commenced, the only snag being a precautionary landing in Greece made necessary by an oil leak. It was registered G-ABLI but the Mailplane failed to win the Air Ministry contract, the winner being the Boulton Paul P.54. After giving a display at Hendon on the 30th August it was flown to Egypt for trials with MISR but these were obviously not a success as it was scrapped in February 1933. The Mailplane, however, formed the basis of a potential passenger plane and a design study was implemented in 1932 which resulted in the Spartan Cruiser I; the wing was the established Avro/Fokker type, very similar to the Cutty Sark incorporating full span box mainspars and plywood skinning. It is a misconception that stressed skin was only introduced with metal construction as in a wood wing the plywood skinning contributes to the overall strength, and as Professor Joad would have said "It all depends upon what you mean by stressed skin". To dispense with the need for longerons the new fuselage was constructed of full length alclad corrugated skinning

attached to dural frames, this technique being much favoured by Saunders Roe in their flying boats. The engines were the same as the Mailplane, namely three 120hp Gipsy III's which gave a cruising speed of 110mph and a top speed of 135mph; the aircraft being fitted out for two crew and six passengers.

The passenger cabin offered exceptional visibility, the side glazing being almost continuous and bore some resemblance to a glass house. This advantage was offset by the method of entry with passengers having to climb onto the wing before entering the cabin via a folding panel on the port side. It was first flown by Lt Col Strange in May 1932 and appeared at the S.B.A.C. show the following month. In October 1932 the Cruiser departed for a sales tour of Europe piloted by the above Lt Col Strange with his wife as one of the passengers. After several stops in Germany the Cruiser gave demonstrations to the Jugoslavian State Airline Aeroput. These included the ability to climb at full load to 2,000ft from take off with one engine shut down; a further in-flight demonstration was given with a payload of 1,000lbs

Cruiser II at Bembridge 1935

Credit: Millichap/Croydon Airport Society

Chief pilot Pat Lynch-Blosse at Bembridge 1933

Credit: Millichap/Croydon Airport Society

Pat Lynch-Blosse at Bembridge 1935

Credit: Millichap/Croydon Airport Society

and with two of the three engines out, which resulted in an altitude loss of about 240ft/per minute. These results impressed the airline and they subsequently ordered two of the later Mark II version plus one to be built under licence, the latter to be powered by Walter Major IV engines of 130hp. Two were also ordered by the Bata shoe company of Zlin, Czechoslavakia. Bata used one of these to make a sales tour of Egypt, the Sudan, South Africa and then back through Africa to Iraq. The homeward leg took the Cruiser over the turbulent and notorious Taurus mountains in Turkey and then home to Zlin. Throughout the 21,000 mile tour the Cruiser's behaviour was excellent with little or no mechanical problems. The Aeroput Cruisers remained in service until the German invasion, as presumably did the Bata Cruisers, but their subsequent fates are unknown. Another Cruiser II was supplied to the Maharaja of Patiala who used it as a personal transport to tour his 99,000 square mile estate.

The prototype Cruiser II received it's Certificate of Airworthiness on 1st February 1933 and had a conventional passenger door on the port side, the cabin windows were re-designed and a vee shape windscreen fitted. The opportunity was taken to improve performance by fitting 130HP Gipsy Major engines giving a cruising speed of 115MPH. Some Cruisers were powered by alternative engines, these being the first aircraft *(C/N 2)* which was operated by Iraq Airwork on the Baghdad - Mosul service being powered by Cirrus Hermes IVs; this aircraft returned to Britain in September 1934 and was taken on the British register as G-ACBM. Two other aircraft were fitted with Walter Major 4 engines, one of which was *(C/N 9)* operated by the Bata Shoe Company and the other, as previously stated, the locally built aircraft in Jugoslavia. The Cruiser was designed to maintain an altitude of 6,000ft with one engine shut down, but this could only have been effective in temperate climates. The passenger cabin, which seated eight, was fitted with royal blue leather seats supplied by Rumbolds. A total of twelve Cruiser IIs were built at Cowes and Spartan Airlines became the main operator. Contemporary photographs show the Cruiser with and without wheel spats.

On the 2nd February 1933, Whitehall Securities formed a separate company, Spartan Airlines with a capital of £10,000 and services commenced on 12th April 1933 from Cowes to Heston utilising the Cruiser I G-ABTY. One month later on the 12th May this aircraft was joined by Cruiser II G-ACDW, thus enabling Spartan to offer a twice daily, including Sundays Cowes - Ryde - Heston service. The initial fares were 38/- *(£1.40)* single and 55/- *(£2.75)* return. Inclusive in the fares was free surface transport between the airways terminal at Victoria Station and Heston Airport; later this was extended to the town centres of Cowes and Ryde to and from their respective airports. The free baggage

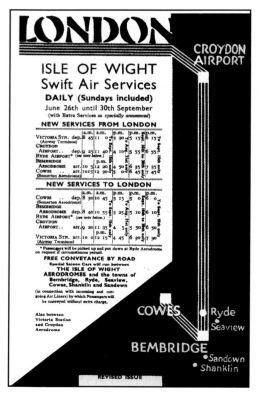

allowance was 30lbs with 2d per pound excess. The service was suspended for the winter on the 2nd October.

On the 9th October 1933 Lord Apsley and Captain Crawford-Greene M.P. for Worcester chartered Spartan Cruiser II G-ACDW for a flight to Australia and in recognition of Worcester's loyalty to the King during the Civil War, the Cruiser was named "Faithful City". On the following morning, flown by Lynch Blosse, it departed the U.K. from Lympne reaching Wyndham on the 27th and Sydney on the 30th. The Cruiser left for home on November 21st with Crawford-Greene leaving at Bombay. The aircraft returned to Britain on Boxing Day having covered some 32,000 miles without incident, thus testifying to the reliability of this Island-built aircraft. Up to that time this was the longest charter ever undertaken by a British, and possibly a World, airline.

At the end of 1933 Spartan AirLines had flown 50,000 miles and carried 1,459 passengers.

The Chief Pilot was P.W. Lynch-Blosse who was born in Glamorgan in 1900. After education at Blundells he served during the latter part of World War I with No 1 Experimental Torpedo Squadron at East Fortune, now the home of the Museum of Flight, a part of the National Museums of Scotland. In the early twenties he first flew for Guinea Airways, New Guinea and then for Australian National Airways as a pilot and instructor. This airline was founded by Kingsford-Smith and Charles Ulm and Lynch-Blosse flew for them from the start of operations. On the 24th April 1921 he piloted the Melbourne - Sydney sector of the first experimental United Kingdom - Australia route in Avro Ten VH-UMG "Southern Star". Five days later he operated the Sydney - Brisbane sector of the above service in another Avro Ten "Southern Sun", but in June of that year the airline went into liquidation and he was out of a job. He moved on to an air survey company operating in the Sudan and Uganda and then came home to be appointed Chief Pilot of Spartan Airlines. He inaugurated the first Cowes - Heston service on the 12th April 1933, which also happened to be his thirty third birthday. He remained with Spartan until it amalgamated with United and Hillman to form British Airways; Lynch-Blosse being appointed Air Superintendent of the new company. He later resigned and joined Qantas Empire Airways and commanded the Short "C" class flying boat VH-ABF "Cooee" on the first Qantas Sydney - Southampton air mail service. At the commencement of hostilities in September 1939 he enlisted in the R.A.F. flying Wellingtons on de-icing and other trials, on the completion of which, he was posted to No 7 Squadron as "A" Flight Commander. He went on to survive a full tour on Stirlings and was awarded the D.F.C. for his attack on Bernberg. After his rest period had expired he was appointed O.C. of 44 Squadron but was killed on the first operation of his second tour.

Another well known individual who flew for Spartan at the beginning was Captain R.H. McIntosh *(all weather Mac)*. He was a First World War pilot who commenced his post War career, firstly with Handley Page, and then with Imperial Airways; as such he was a contemporary of Gordon Olley *(see chapter on Channel Air Ferries)*. His nickname of "all weather Mac" was coined in 1921 when inbound to Croydon in very murky conditions his trailing aerial snagged on a tree and was carried away thus depriving

Pilots of Spartan Airlines left to right:
Halliwell, Macintosh, Lynch-Blosse and van Oppen

Credit: Tom Hiett

him of the ability to transmit or receive. He could, however, see the towers of Crystal Palace and from experience knew the exact heading to the airport where he made a perfectly normal landing. The passengers were not informed about the mishap with the trailing aerial, but one of them was the Editor of the
'Daily Chronicle' and next morning the paper printed an article extolling the virtues of wireless telegraphy! In 1938 he worked for Martin's at Shoreham which had a contract for navigational training with the R.A.F. Martins being equipped with a Dragon and several Dragon Rapides, all aircraft being modified with a drift sight set in the floor and a chart table. Two R.A.F. pupils were accommodated but the pilots and radio officers were civilians. During the War McIntosh joined the R.A.F. and became a Wing Commander.

1934

In reply to previous conversations between Harold Balfour M.C., M.P., a Director of Spartan and Woods Humphery Managing Director of Imperial Airways, the latter wrote to the former on the 21st February advising him that Imperial are forming an internal airline in conjunction with the four railway companies and as such precluded Imperial from co-operating with Whitehall Securities. Woods Humphery did indicate that the Southern Railway could be interested in co-operating with Spartan on their Isle of Wight services and would approach them without delay. This resulted in a meeting between Harold Balfour and Sir Herbert Walker, Chief General Manager of the Southern Railway. the outcome of which was that for the twelve months commencing 1st May 1934 the two companies would share equally in the income and expenses to a limit of 1,640 flights at a maximum cost per flight of £5-18-0 (£5.90). It was not intended that the railway would invest by way of share capital and hopefully this disposes of the myth which has grown over the years that the Southern Railway subscribed to equity. While these matters were being discussed the four railways held meetings with a view to entering air transport and this culminated in a decision to form Railway Air Services Ltd, which was incorporated on the 21st March 1934. Each of the railway companies *(including the Southern)* held 20% with Imperial Airways holding the remaining 20%. When the other railways discovered that the Southern had made a separate agreement with Spartan they were somewhat perturbed, as they saw it as violating the spirit of the Railway Air Service arrangements. On the 30th April 1934 the R.A.S. board recorded

Spartan Airlines Transport. Driver: 'Wink'.   Credit: Millichap/Croydon Airport Society

Spartan Airlines bus and car at Somerton   Credit: Millichap/Croydon Airport Society

disapproval and on the same day Sir Harold Hartley, the Chairman of R.A.S. and deputy Chairman of the L.M.S., wrote to the Southern expressing the board's dismay, but of no avail as the Southern Railway/Spartan service commenced the next day! This must have been a considerable embarrassment to Imperial Airways given that they introduced the parties involved.

It will be noted that the 1934 timetable is headed "Southern Air Services" with the word "Southern" being in identical style to that of the Southern Railway. The alliance with the Southern Railway gave Spartan a marketing and ticketing advantage as bookings could be made at all major stations; this being later extended to virtually all stations including all those on the Island. In addition, passengers holding return

tickets had the option of returning to London by first class rail travel. Services commenced on the 1st May and the London terminal transferred from Heston to Croydon. The Croydon - Ryde - Cowes route was operated at frequencies of up to five times daily including Sundays. Bembridge was advertised as a request stop if "inducement offers and circumstances permit". The fares at the beginning of the season were 30/- *(£1.50)* single and 50/- *(£2.50)* return but unlike 1933 when Spartan had the monopoly of the London - Island route, competition appeared in the form of Portsmouth based PSIOWA who on the same day that Spartan started their 1934 services , the company opened a Heston - Ryde route with fares being only 19/6 *(97p)* single and 38/6 return *(£1.92)*, these, in fact, being identical to the first class train fare. Spartan must have been hurt by this as on the 26th June they were forced to match fares, these new lower fares still included free surface transport from and to Victoria and Croydon. The Cruiser II had now been operated for a year and A. & A.E.E. were persuaded to increase the maximum take off weight from 5,700lbs to 6,200lbs, which in theory meant it could carry ten passengers but it would have been very cramped. During the 1934 peak periods demand was such that at times Spartan were forced to charter a twenty seat Armstrong Whitworth Argosy II G-AACJ "City of Manchester" from Imperial Airways. The normal route for these aircraft was from Croydon to Basle and Salonika and, for its time, the Argosy was very luxurious. They inaugurated the Imperial Airways much patronised upmarket London - Paris "Silver Wing" service and while on charter to Spartan "City of Manchester" was flown by R.H. McIntosh who had piloted the type when he was with Imperial Airways.

In the early 1930's a Mr Millichap who worked for the Southern Railway had a son, Ray, who was interested in aviation and through his connections managed to obtain for him an introduction to Spartan Airlines Ltd. His first job, which was unpaid, was to cycle six miles from his home in Bembridge to Ryde Airport, peer through the hedge, and note the number of passengers arriving and departing on the PSIOWA services, the result being reported at the end of each day. In 1934 he was interviewed by Lynch-Bosse who appointed him Traffic Manager at Bembridge, but despite the title he was, in effect, a general factotum. His duties comprised of looking after passengers, refuelling, preparing the ships papers and propeller swinging. The appointment called for working from dawn to dusk during the summer for seven days a week, the pay being 10/- *(50p)* per day. He was later transferred to Cowes and then when Spartan became part of British Airways he was posted first to Croydon and then to Heston. At the latter airport he prepared the ships papers for Chamberlain's "Peace in our time" flight to Munich. He was then posted as Station Manager at Paris followed by Budapest and finally Berlin. On the outbreak of War he and the resident engineer managed to escape by enduring sixty hour journey in an old train to Athens and then to Alexandria and from there to Poole in an Imperial Airways "C" class flying boat. Upon his return he was reprimanded for incurring the cost of his escape as being improper and unauthorised use of company funds! During the War he joined the R.A.F. and after three years of instructing he was posted to 207 and then to 630 Squadron, both Squadrons being equipped with Lancasters. He completed an operational tour of thirty three missions and was awarded the D.F.C. Three days after the War ended, he was seconded to B.O.A.C. On the 4th October 1958 he flew Comet "Delta Charlie" from London to New York as Captain Tom Stoney simultaneously flew another Comet from New York to London, thus inaugurating the first trans Atlantic Jet service and beating Pan Am by twenty two days. He retired from B.O.A.C. in 1965

Preparing for helicopter lift   Credit: Museum of Flight East Fortune
25 July 1973 to Museum of Flight East Fortune

RAILWAY AIR SERVICES
SPARTAN AIR LINES

Daily services by Multi-engined Air Liners
BETWEEN

GATWICK AIRPORT
AND
ISLE OF WIGHT

Ryde Airport (with road conveyance to and from Seaview, Bembridge, Sandown and Shanklin), Somerton Airport (with road conveyance to and from Cowes)

SPECIAL FARES FROM AND TO GATWICK
(including Road Transport in Isle of Wight)

SINGLE	ORDINARY RETURN
25/-	**45/-** (available one month)

SPECIAL MID-WEEK PERIOD RETURN
35/-
Available outwards Tuesday, Wednesday or Thursday to return on any Tuesday, Wednesday or Thursday within one Calendar Month.

DAY EXCURSION RETURN TICKET
30/-
Issued for travel from Gatwick on Mondays, Tuesdays, Wednesdays, Thursdays or Fridays ; from Isle of Wight on Tuesdays, Wednesdays, Thursdays. Available for return on same day only.

CHILDREN
In arms up to 3 years of age free, if not occupying separate seat. 3 and under 7 years, half full fares. 7 years and over, full fares.

GATWICK AIRPORT is adjacent to the specially constructed Railway Station served by frequent Southern Electric trains and affording connection from and to Horley, Redhill, Three Bridges, Balcombe, Crawley, Horsham, East Grinstead and Tunbridge Wells.

TERMS AND CONDITIONS OF CARRIAGE
The Conditions under which British Airways Ltd. (the contracting Air Company) undertakes to carry passengers and baggage may be inspected at any aerodrome used by the Company.

FOR TIME TABLE SEE FOLDER obtainable at GATWICK AIR-PORT (Phone Crawley 600) and SOUTHERN RLY. STATIONS

RAS/Spartan Dragon at Somerton 1936

Credit: John King

Spartan Cruiser III G-ACYK at Largs 14 January 1938

Credit: Museum of Flight East Fortune

and became an Air Accident Investigator and finally a C.A.A. Operations Inspector. He died in 1995 aged 79. After Millichip joined Spartan at Bembridge the Railway appointed a parcel porter at Sandown as their new spy at Ryde Airport. His name was Ron Anderson who was instructed that at the end of each day he was to telegraph the numbers to the Superintendent of the Southern Railway at Woking.

The summer schedules ceased on the 30th September and from the 1st October to the 31st the frequency was reduced to twice per weekday and one on Sundays. The weekdays only flights called at Southampton for connections via R.A.S. to the Midlands and the North and via Jersey

Airways for the Channel Islands. Although the agreement with the Southern Railway was for twelve months commencing May 1st, the constraining fact was the actual number of flights and as the railway did not subsidise flights after the 31st October it must be assumed that the 1,640 flights had been completed. From that date Spartan operated a winter service on its own account with one service per day, the exception being the four day Christmas period when it was increased to two.

During the year Spartan Aircraft embarked upon a re-design of the Cruiser, this version becoming known as the Cruiser III. This differed from the earlier models, with the dispensing of the slab sided fuselage in favour of a longer and more aerodynamically efficient shape, an enlarged fin and rudder and a fully trousered undercarriage. This version was fitted with the same Gipsy Major engines of the Cruiser II, these improvements giving a slightly higher cruising speed of 118MPH. Only three were built, the first G-ACYK *(C/N 101)* entering service with Spartan Airlines in April 1935.

1934 saw a considerable improvement in traffic with 6,709 passengers being carried which equated to a load factor of 70% and a regularity of 99.71%, only five flights being cancelled due to weather. There was a recognised bad weather route which, after taking off from Ryde, was to locate the forts in Spithead, fly along the Sussex coast until the main railway line came into view which was then followed to Gatwick and from there through a gap in the downs to Croydon. When all other aircraft were grounded "All weather Mac" could normally be relied upon to appear out of the overcast sky and land!

1935

As a consequence of Railway Air Services substituting Portsmouth instead of the Island on the Liverpool - Shoreham service, a Southampton - Cowes - Sandown ferry service was started with six return flights per day during the week and four on Sunday with some flights connecting with the Railway Air Services service at Southampton. During August the frequency was increased to eight services per day.

The Airline was now advertised as Railway Air Services-Spartan AirLines. A de Havilland Dragon II was used on the Island - Southampton ferry but there is some confusion over its identity. John Stroud, in his book 'Railway Air Services', states that it was G-ACNI which belonged to Jersey Airways. Both 'British Civil Aircraft' volume II *(Putnams)* and Neville Doyle in 'Sea Eagle to Flamingo' show this aircraft in service with Jersey Airways during 1935 and was not sold to British Airways, Eastleigh until February 1936. Certainly during 1936 it operated the Gatwick - Island route. The other possible aircraft could have been G-ACNG and this was definitely in possession of Spartan Airlines from June 1935. It could well be that all sources are correct in respect of G-ACNI as it may have been chartered from Jersey Airways in which case no change of ownership would have been shown.

The Cruiser I G-ABTY which had inaugurated the first service in April 1933 was sold in February to the Hon. Mrs Victor Bruce. It was operated by Commercial Air Hire Ltd *(later Air Despatch Ltd)* on early morning newspaper runs to France and on the 11th May while engaged upon these duties it ditched in the Channel off le Tréport. Before the start of the season the London terminal reverted to Heston from Croydon. The service commenced on the 14th April and was now promoted as Railway Air Services - Spartan Airlines.

The frequency of services varied according to the day of the

LONDON—ISLE OF WIGHT.	**Summer Time Table.**		1st July—15th September.

Direct Service to and from Sandown (for Shanklin).   Via Heston Airport.

	MONDAY				TUESDAY WEDNESDAY THURSDAY (A)			FRIDAY				SATURDAY					SUNDAY		
FROM LONDON	a.m.	a.m.	p.m.	p.m.	a.m.	a.m.	p.m.	a.m.	a.m.	p.m.	p.m.	a.m.	a.m.	p.m.	p.m.	p.m.	a.m.	p.m.	p.m.
By road VICTORIA STATION *dep.*	8-30	11- 0	1-15	6- 0	8-30	11- 0	6- 0	8-30	11- 0	3-30	6- 0	8-30	11- 0	1-15	3-30	6- 0	10- 0	3-30	6- 0
„ HESTON ... ... *arr.*	9-15	11-45	2- 0	6-45	9-15	11-45	6-45	9-15	11-45	4-15	6-45	9-15	11-45	2- 0	4-15	6-45	10-45	4-15	6-45
By air HESTON ... ... *dep.*	9-25	11-55	2-10	6-55	9-25	11-55	6-55	9-25	11-55	4-25	6-55	9-25	11-55	2-10	4-25	6-55	10-55	4-25	6-55
„ SANDOWN ... ... *arr.*	10-10	12-40	2-55	7-40	10-10	12-40	7-40	10-10	12-40	5-10	7-40	10-10	12-40	2-55	5-10	7-40	11-40	5-10	7-40
TO LONDON.																			
By air SANDOWN ... *dep.*	8-30	11- 0	1-15	6- 0	8-30	11- 0	6- 0	8-30	11- 0	3-30	6- 0	8-30	11- 0	1-15	3-30	6- 0	10- 0	3-30	6- 0
„ HESTON ... ... *arr.*	9-15	11-45	2- 0	6-45	9-15	11-45	6-45	9-15	11-45	4-15	6-45	9-15	11-45	2- 0	4-15	6-45	10-45	4-15	6-45
By road HESTON ... ... *dep.*	9-20	11-50	2- 5	6-50	9-20	11-50	6-50	9-20	11-50	4-20	6-50	9-20	11-50	2- 5	4-20	6-50	10-50	4-20	6-50
„ VICTORIA STATION *arr.*	10- 0	12-35	2-50	7-35	10- 0	12-35	7-35	10- 0	12-35	5- 5	7-35	10- 0	12-35	2-50	5- 5	7-35	11-35	5- 5	7-35

(A)—This service will NOT operate during July and September.

Passengers to and from Bembridge, Cowes, Ryde and Seaview must travel on the Bembridge—Cowes service.

Passengers to and from Sandown and Shanklin must take direct Sandown service when service is provided.

SPECIAL ROAD TRANSPORT IS PROVIDED **FREE** BETWEEN AIRPORTS AND ABOVE PLACES.

Cruiser II G-ACDW at Cairo

Credit: Mike Hooks

week with up to five flights per day Fridays and Saturdays. During the peak period, and to cater for weekenders, a late Sunday evening service was introduced leaving Cowes at 20.05 and Bembridge ten minutes later, arriving at Heston at 20.55 and Victoria Station at 21.45. The free baggage allowance was now 35lbs and the fares were 26/6 *(£1.32)* single and 45/- *(£2.25)* return. As in previous years the fare included coach travel from and to Victoria and the airport. On the Island company cars at no extra charge were provided from Ryde, Seaview, Bembridge, Shanklin and Sandown. The pick up and set down points were:- Bembridge - Central garage, Seaview - Watson Brothers, Ryde - Esplanade Station, Sandown - 59 High Street and at Shanklin the Railway Station.

On the 1st July an entirely new route was opened, this being a direct Heston - Sandown service which operated in addition to the existing Heston - Bembridge - Cowes route. In July the new Sandown service operated only on Mondays *(4 flights)*, Fridays *(4 flights)*, Saturdays *(5 flights)* and Sundays *(3 flights)*, but commencing August there were daily services with the minimum of three per day. From the 1st September until the 15th, when the service closed, the schedule was as in July. The fares were identical to the main route.

During the period of 29th April to 31st December 1935 Spartan operated 1,375 flights with a total mileage of 99,305 miles and incurred an operating loss of £3,694. Interestingly, travel agents situated on the Island were paid 10% commission whereas those on the mainland only received

71/2 %! The exceptions to this were the major agents such as Thomas Cook, Pickfords, Dean and Dawson and Amex who once their bookings exceeded £300 they were paid 10% on the full amount.

The basic problem for Spartan was that at weekends there was only one way traffic with flights from London being full on Fridays and Saturdays but returning empty; on Sundays and Mondays the reverse was true and although this pattern also affected PSIOWA on their Heston - Island route they were cushioned by the Portsmouth - Ryde ferry, Spartan not having this back-up. It was not unusual on peak Saturdays for a number of Cruisers to take off from Heston in quick succession and for the entertainment of passengers to fly in formation.

On the 9th October Spartan suffered their one and only serious accident. Spartan Cruiser II G-ACDX 'Hampshire' departed Blackpool for Cowes with a stop at Heston. On the Heston - Cowes sector the only occupant was the pilot, Captain R.H. McIntosh (All Weather Mac). Upon crossing the coast at Gosport, he experienced total failure of all three engines and rather than risk ditching, he turned back and tried to reach R.A.F. Fort Grange at Gosport, but crashed into the garden of Colonel O.C. Downes of the 1st Battalion, the Rifle Brigade. McIntosh was only slightly hurt, but the Colonel was somewhat peeved at the damage to his rhododendrons!

During the 1930s there were about thirty internal airlines in Britain of which some twelve were placed in liquidation. The key to survival meant more robust financing and amalgamation. Whitehall Securities had very substantial stakes in Spartan, United Airlines (itself an amalgamate of Highland and Island Airways and Northern and Scottish Airlines) and British Continental Airways. It was estimated that by merging Spartan and United substantial savings could be made, particularly if Hillman Airways could be brought into the fold. This latter company being owned by another finance house, d'Erlangers. Agreement was reached between the parties and a new company was formed on the 30th September 1935 named Allied British Airways. A month later "Allied" was deleted and the company became just plain British Airways with a capital of £245,240. It was agreed that the constituent airlines would retain their individual titles until January 1937 after which they would operate under the banner of British Airways.
During the period October 1935 to January 1936 the Cowes - Bembridge - Heston service was reduced to one return flight per weekday with two on Saturdays. An out by air and home by rail was available at 35/- *(£1.75)* First Class and 30/- *(£1.50)* Third Class.

The passenger figures show a substantial drop over 1934 (1934: 6,708) to 4,463. Spartan's operations produced a loss of £7,388 on a route mileage of 99,305 and 1,375 flights. As the number of flights were within the 1,640 contracted with the Southern Railway, the loss was split between them.

1936

By the beginning of 1936 nearly all the Cruisers had been transferred to the Northern routes which left the Spartan division of British Airways shorn of aircraft but an agreement was reached between the Southern Railway and British Airways to operate a service to the Island from Gatwick commencing on the 25th May until the 3rd October. The route was to be operated by two ex-Jersey Airways de Havilland 84 Dragons G-ACNI and G-ACNG and at peak periods there were up to nine departures to the Island per day and eight return flights. The fares were 25/- single *(£1.25)* and 45/- return *(£2.25)* with a special day return of 30/- *(£1.50)* and a mid-week return of 35/- *(£1.75)* valid up to one month. These fares were subsequently increased to 30/- single *(£1.50)*, 50/- monthly return *(£2.50)*, 33/- day return *(£1.65)* and mid-week monthly return 40/- *(£2.00)*.

Gatwick was chosen as the operational headquarters of British Airways and the advantages to them and the Southern Railway were such it was decided to give it a trial. Gatwick was on the Southern's main Victoria - Brighton line and was the first mainline, as opposed to local lines, to be electrified and the local station known as Tinsley Green was renamed Gatwick Airport. it has been claimed that Gatwick was the first airport in the country to have a station but this is not so as Shoreham had Bungalow Town Halt *(later Shoreham Airport)* which had been there many years, Shoreham was the oldest licenced airport in the country having been established in 1911. One should also mention Southampton and Portsmouth who had mainlines adjacent to the airports, both of which pre dated Gatwick.

A complete re-organisation of the Isle of Wight route was undertaken with dead mileage being ruthlessly pruned. This resulted in only Gatwick - Ryde - Cowes being operated, the direct Sandown route was dropped, as was the Island - Southampton service which was left to R.A.S. and PSIOWA. Offices were required at Ryde Airport and after some negotiation on terms agreement was reached with the owners Vectis Airports Ltd *(a subsidiary of PSIOWA)*. The timetable for 1936 provided for 817 flights and a total aircraft mileage of 48,977 *(1935 - 1,375 flights and 99,305 miles)*. Ground transport from Shanklin, Sandown, Bembridge, Seaview to Ryde also Cowes *(Somerton)* to Cowes town was inclusive as was the train fare from London to Gatwick. Up to now the Spartan standard return was valid for three months but in 1936 with the purpose of bringing it into line with railway practice the validity was reduced to one month. After taking into account ancillary charges such as airport costs, train and road transport, publicity etc; the single air fare of 25/- *(£1.25)* was effectively reduced to 18/- *(90p)* but it was hoped that the Dragons would show some operating economies as they had the same passenger capacity as the Cruisers, but only two instead of three engines. The board estimated that the loss for the year should not exceed £2,000 each for the Southern Railway and British Airways. An illuminating comment made was that "The nett loss of operating the route must be regarded as expenditure for policy reasons".

In the period of 25th May to 3rd October passengers carried were 2,964 and from the latter date Spartan ceased operations forever.

Note:- The passengers carried figures are at variance with certain other sources but the figures quoted are from the records of Mr Harrington, a Southern Railway manager, who was appointed as Liaison Manager to Spartan. These figures were the ones presented by him to the board of the Southern Railway and as such can be considered accurate. the periods in question are:-

	1934
1st May - 31st October 1934	6,799
	1935
29th April - 3rd December 1935	4,463
	1936
25th May - 3rd October 1936	2,964

Aircraft of Spartan Airlines & their Fates

Spartan Cruiser I G-ABTY

Delivered 16th August 1932, sold to Hon. Mrs V Bruce in February 1935. On the 11th May 1935 while operated by Commercial Air Hire on an early morning newspaper run, it ditched in the Channel off Le Tréport.

Spartan Cruiser II G-ACBM

Delivered to Airwork Ltd in February 1933 who operated it in Iraq as YI-AAA for pioneering a potential air route between Baghdad and Mosul. Upon return in 1934, it was taken over by Spartan Airlines for normal service. After the absorption of Spartan by British Airways, it came into the hands of the Straight Corporation who scrapped it in November 1937. This aircraft was powered by Hermes IV engines instead of the usual Gipsy Majors.

Spartan Cruiser II G-ACDW

Delivered 12th May 1933 and was the first Cruiser II to operate the Spartan routes. Sold to MISR (Egyptian Airlines) but operated by Airwork Ltd. Used on the Cairo - Jerusalem - Haifa route. Fate unknown.

Cruiser II G-ACDX 'Hampshire'

Delivered 19th June 1933. on 9th October 1935 while bound for Cowes from Heston, this aircraft suffered fuel starvation and crashed at Gosport

Cruiser II G-ACSM 'Sussex'

Delivered June 1934. Sent north in August 1936 to operate with Northern and Scottish Airways. This aircraft may have been loaned to United Airways during 1935 (United were the parent company of Northern and Scottish Airlines and Highland and Islands Airways). Impressed into RAF April 1940 but scrapped in July.

Cruiser II G-ACVT

Delivered 2nd August 1934. Transferred to British Airways in February 1936 to work the Isle of Man routes but crashed at Ronaldsway (Isle of Man) on 23rd March.

Spartan Cruiser II G-ACZM

Delivered 13th December 1934. Transferred to British Airways in january 1936 for use on the North of England and Scottish routes. Scrapped April 1942.

Cruiser III G-ACYK

Delivered 16th April 1935. Transferred to British Airways April 1936 but continued to operate Spartan routes until August when transferred to north of England for the Scottish routes. Crashed near Largs 14th January 1938. The cabin section was lifted from the hills by Royal Navy helicopter in July 1973 and taken to the Museum of Flight, East Fortune where it resides today.

Cruiser III G-ADEL

Delivered 18th April 1935. Transferred to British Airways October 1936 for use on the north of England and Scottish routes. Impressed by the RAF April 1940 but scrapped in July of the same year.

Cruiser II G-ADEM

Delivered 3rd June 1935. Transferred to British Airways April 1936 for use on the North of England and Scottish routes. Hit hanger on take off in fog at Blackpool (Stanley Park) 20th November 1936 - two killed.

Spartan three seater II G-ABTR

Delivered 2nd June 1932. This aircraft was certainly based at Cowes and probably used for local joy-riding. Sold to a F. G. Barnard of Hayling Island on September 1937. Part of a number of derelict aircraft which were burnt at Gatwick in 1947. Twenty five of these aircraft were built but this was the only example with an enclosed cabin.

de Havilland Dragon II G-ACNG

Ex Jersey Airways, transferred to Spartan in June 1935 and to the new British Airways in March 1936 (a paper transfer). It is very likely that this aircraft operated in the livery of 'Railway Air Services'. In January 1937 it was transferred to Northern and Scottish Airlines. Crashed Kirkwall on the 19th April 1940.

Armstrong Whitworth Argosy

G-AAJ 'City of Manchester

During 1934 and 1935it was chartered on an 'ad hoc' basis from Imperial Airways. Powered by three Armstrong Siddeley Jaguar IVA engines each of 420HP, with accommodation for two pilots and twenty passengers. By removing the two rear passenger seats a buffet and a steward could be carried.

Brief Specifications of Spartan Cruisers Mark I, II and III

CRUISER I

Power Plant	3 X 120HP Gipsy III
Wingspan	54' 0"
Length	39' 2"
Maximum all up weight	5,500lbs
Maximum speed	135 MPH
Cruising speed	110 MPH
Range	660 miles
Accommodation	2 crew + up to 6 passengers

CRUISER II

Power Plant	3 X 130HP Gipsy Majors
Wingspan	54' 0"
Length	39' 2"
Maximum all up weight	6,200lbs
Maximum speed	133 MPH
Cruising speed	115 MPH
Range	310 miles
Accommodation	2 crew + up to 8 passengers

CRUISER III

Power Plant	3 X 130HP Gipsy Majors
Wingspan	54' 0"
Length	41' 0"
Maximum all up weight	6,200lbs
Maximum speed	135 MPH
Cruising speed	118 MPH
Range	550 miles
Accommodation	2 crew + up to 8 passengers

FLEET

1933

Spartan Cruiser II	G-ACDX "Hampshire"	Crashed 9th October

1934

Spartan Cruiser II	G-ACSM	
Spartan Cruiser II	G-ACUT	To British Airways in October
Spartan Cruiser II	G-ACYL	To United Airlines in April
Spartan Cruiser II	G-ACZM	To British Airways in October

April 1935

Spartan Cruiser III	G-ACYK	To British Airways in October
Spartan Cruiser III	G-ADEL	To British Airways in October

June 1935

Spartan Cruiser III	G-ADEM	To British Airways in October

Railway Air Services

Railway Air Services was a very significant, and indeed possibly the largest operator of internal air services before World War II, but this book is only concerned with their operations that serviced the Isle of Wight. Any reader who wishes to study the activities of R.A.S. in other parts of the country should try and obtain a copy of 'Railway Air Services' by John Stroud and published in 1987 by Ian Allan Ltd.

It can be considered that the period from the middle of the nineteenth century to the commencement of the second World War, the advent of the Railways with their developing mass transport system were largely responsible for the greatest social and industrial revolution in the history of Great Britain. They were instrumental in creating a hitherto non existent market for travel within the means of the ordinary person. This was further encouraged by the marketing of cheap day and excursion fares. During the First World War tremendous calls were made on the railway system and under the resultant pressure the permanent way, signalling and rolling stock suffered. Britain emerged from the War with a multitude of railway companies, many on the brink of bankruptcy, and to avoid any possible chaos the Government introduced legislation which resulted in the Railway Grouping Act of 1921. The Act required the new "Big Four" to take over all lines in their designated areas and this became effective as from 1st January 1923.

The Southern Railway had the task of absorbing its constituent companies which included the London and South Western, London, Brighton and South Coast, the South Eastern, the London Chatham and Dover and the South Eastern and Chatham.

In addition to these mainland companies the Isle of Wight companies also had to be brought into the fold, these being the Isle of Wight Central Railway, the Isle of Wight Railway and the Freshwater, Yarmouth and Newport. these three being an amalgamation of the original six Island railways which had a combined route mileage of 45.25 miles! The last named was not taken over until the 1st August 1923 as the Southern was reluctant to accept their very few assets and many liabilities but were forced to do so by the Government. With designs of new locomotives on the drawing board the upgrading of permanent way, signalling

Railway Air Services Dragon G-ACNI   Credit: Science Museum/Science & Society Library

Avro Tudor G-ABZP at Cowes, 1935   Credit: Barry Price

etc became a priority and this combined with the management time devoted to the mergers was instrumental in the railways overlooking the steady but remorseless rise in road transport and became alarmed at the inroads being made by this largely unregulated and formidable competitor. They were not prepared to stand by and see this "Johnny come lately" steal their market and therefore by intensive Parliamentary lobbying, they were successful in being granted powers to operate road transport under the Railways *(Road Transport)* Act of 1928.

As far as the Isle of Wight is concerned, the Southern Railway was in a strong position as not only did they operate the railways on both the mainland and the Island but also the connecting steamships that plied between Portsmouth and Ryde and Lymington to Yarmouth *(the Southampton - Cowes service was operated by an independent company, the Southampton, Isle of Wight and South of England Royal Mail Steam Packet Company Ltd).*

Not content with this, on the 1st March 1929, the Southern acquired 50% of Island Bus Operators, Dodson Brothers and on the 27th August of the same year this became a limited company named "Southern Vectis Omnibus Company Ltd", with a nominal capital of £150.000, the head office transferred to Waterloo Station, and this combined with the Chairman being a Director of the Southern gave the railway effective control. By this means the Southern Railway had therefore achieved that most desirable objective of any transport operator namely an "All through" integrated system.

'City of Bristol' at Ryde   Credit: Philip Jarrett

Although in the late 1920's internal air transport was virtually non existent in this country, France and Germany had created comprehensive networks of air services and the railways were determined no to be caught out a second time. Having won a belated right to operate road transport the railways managed to have two Bills passed through Parliament which were known as Railways *(Air Transport)* Bills, the stated intention being "That they be at liberty to take a share in the inevitable development of air transport and avoid a repetition of their experience with road transport". The Bills became law on the 5th May 1929.

Avro Club Cadet at Sandown. 1935   Credit: Barry Price

Sir Herbert Walker, the Chief General Manager of the Southern Railway had a far sighted but hard nosed attitude, not only to the railways, but to other forms of transport and during his term in office he instituted (for its day) sophisticated reporting systems and other techniques which made the Southern one of the more efficient railways of the time. According the "The Times", "He knew what the public wanted and had the vision and will to scrap old ideas and old ways to make these things possible". Although the Southern Railway route structure was, in general, too short to be adversely affected by air transport they considered that their long established rail - steamship - rail service from London to Paris to be under serious threat from Imperial Airways and in order to protect this asset, and before the railways were granted powers to operate air services, the Southern started buying up shares in Imperial. When they had acquired 20% they opened negotiations with a view to persuade Imperial to sell them their Paris and Brussels services and from 1929 onward the Southern became the largest single shareholder in Imperial. Under the Act of 1929, the Southern Railway was allowed to operate air services as far away as Iceland, Portugal, Norway and Sweden but in the case of the latter country only to the south of the Gulf of Bothnia. They were authorised to carry mails

Cierva Autogiro at Cowes, 1935   Credit: Barry Price

as required by the Postmaster General and also to purchase land and buildings for airfields. It had always been railway practice to have their own facilities for the design and construction of locomotives and rolling stock but under the provisions of Act they were precluded from the manufacture of aircraft and engines or having any financial interest in any company engaged in this field.

The Southern was unsuccessful in obtaining the Imperial Airways Paris and Brussels routes but an agreement was reached whereby the railways would only charter air services from Imperial and in return the Southern Railway would receive preferential treatment. In 1933 it came to the notice of the Southern Railway Board that the Great Western Railway were considering starting an air service and this galvanised the Southern Railway to set up a committee under the Chairmanship of G.W. Erskine Loder *(later Lord Wakehurst)* to study how air transport could benefit the railways. At a fee of £2,500 the Committee appointed the consultants Norman, Muntz and Dawbarn to investigate and report. Sir Josiah Stamp, Chairman of the London, Midland and Scottish Railways stated "The railways are not going to sit back and let the airlines rob them of their traffic". The

Railway Air Services Dragon at Portsmouth

Credit: 'The News' Portsmouth

Railway Air Services Dragon G-ADDI at Bristol

Credit: Philip Jarrett

consultants report was received in early March 1934 and in order to discuss the implications, the Southern convened a meeting with the other three railways and Imperial Airways; the outcome of which was the formation of Railway Air Services Ltd with an authorised capital of £50,000. The company was registered on the 24th of the same month with each of the four railways holding 20% and Imperial Airways subscribing for the remaining 20%.

The initial Board consisted of Sir Harold Hartley, Chairman *(representing the L.M.S.),* O.H. Corble *(L.N.E.R.),* S.B. Collett *(G.W.R.),* G.S. Szlumper *(S.R.)* and Lt Col H. Burchall *(Imperial Airways).* It was agreed that Imperial Airways would supply flight crews and technical services and an executive of Imperial Airways, Wing Commander A.H. Measures, was appointed Superintendent. The financial arrangements were that Railway Air Services Ltd would pass

all the receipts to the Railway Companies who in return would pay all operating expenses. An added incentive for the railways to operate air services was a letter from Mr Woods Humphrey, Managing Director of Imperial Airways which was read out at the Railway General Manager's Conference of 1933 and which stated "My colleagues, like yourselves, foresee that internal air communications in this country might get into a confused state unless services are organised in such a way which will prevent haphazard and possibly unsatisfactory services being started in all directions. To avoid overlapping and to concentrate resources and experience into as strong an organisation as possible, some co-operative effort between the railway companies seems likely to give the best results".

This statement could well be interpreted as diplomatic language for an attempt to achieve a monopoly as Imperial

Airways were already the Government's "Chosen Instrument" to operate the Continental and Empire routes while their partners Railway Air Services were to work the internal services. The very first example of a railway being involved with an air service was in April of the previous year when the Great Western started an experimental service between Cardiff and Haldon *(Torquay)* and later extended to Birmingham and Plymouth. The aircraft was a Westland Wessex G-AAGW which was painted in the standard G.W.R. rolling stock livery of chocolate and cream and was chartered from Imperial Airways who also supplied staff and technical support. As this route did not involve the Isle of Wight it is not of direct concern and further details may be found in John Stroud's "Railway Air Services".

In early 1934 Captain Balfour (later Lord Balfour of Inchrye), Chairman of Spartan Airlines Ltd, held a meeting with Sir Herbert Walker armed with a proposal that the Southern Railway participate in their Cowes - London service which had commenced operating in April of the previous year. Spartan Airlines was part of Whitehall Securities, an investment company which in turn was a subsidiary of the influential Pearson Group, the Managing Director of which was the Hon Clive Pearson, who was later to become a director of the Southern Railway! An agreement was reached whereby for the twelve months commencing 1st May 1934 the Southern and Spartan would share equally in the receipts and expenses of the operation, income being projected as £6,796 and expenses of £9,696 leaving a loss of £2,880. It was not intended that the Southern would put up any share capital and the details were that for the twelve months in question there would be 1,640 flights at a maximum cost per flight of £5.18.0 *(£5.90)*. Several sources claim that the Southern Railway acquired 50% of the share capital but this was patently not so. This arrangement caused consternation with the other shareholders of R.A.S. but more of this in the chapter on Spartan Airlines. The railways informed all travel agents that if they booked passengers with other airlines, apart from Imperial Airways or airlines approved by the railways, they would be banned from transacting any business in respect of rail or sea journeys. This had the effect of tying the agents to R.A.S. and Spartan to the detriment of other operators, thus giving R.A.S. and associated airlines an unfair advantage. Even after a total of twenty one questions had been asked in Parliament, no action was taken by the Government until 1938 resulting in the railways having to discontinue the scheme.

As a result of an in depth study of the types of aircraft available and with a strong recommendation from Imperial Airways, Railway Air Services Ltd *(RAS)* approached de Havilland with the intention of placing an order for two of their new Dragon Rapides, but due to demand the order could not be fulfilled for twelve months. In order to keep to

Credit: Welsh Industrial and Maritime Museum

the proposed start-up date they chartered two de Havilland 84 Series II Dragons, one from the manufacturer *(G-ACPX)* and the other from Olley Air Services *(G-ACPY)*.

The Dragon was a two bay biplane of conventional construction and powered by two Gipsy Major engines each of 130hp, giving a cruising speed of 114mph. It was, in fact, a twin engine version of the Fox Moth and was designed from the outset for the utmost of economy and maintenance, the wings outboard of the engines being standard Fox Moth and for the ease of storage these could be folded. Another feature was a zip fastener under the fuselage which gave easy access to the control runs. It is often stated that Edward Hillman of Hillman Airways was the instigator of the design and whilst it is true that he was the first British operator, the original motivation came from the Iraqi Air Force who wanted a twin engine light bomber de Havilland did, in fact, supply the Iraqis with eight aircraft, these being equipped with racks to carry sixteen 20lb bombs plus a mid upper gun position.

The version used by Railway Air Services was the Series II which was equipped with wheel spats and framed passenger windows which replaced the continuous glazing of the previous Series. The economics exceeded even those of the Fox Moth with a fuel consumption as low as 13 gallons per hour, the Gipsy engines proving very reliable resulting in an overhaul cycle of 750 flying hours with no interim top overhauls. With a wing loading at maximum all up weight of 4,500lbs of 12lbs/sq ft the Dragon was light but provided the approach speed did not exceed 65mph the aircraft would get down and stay down. The take off run to unstick was 220yds and the corresponding landing of only 130yds. The capital cost of the Dragon in 1934 was £2,950 and there is little doubt that it produced the lowest operating costs of any aircraft in its class, 70 Dragons being operated by British Airlines. A total of 115 were built in this country plus 87 in Australia. In normal service the Dragon could accommodate up to eight passengers but on short routes up to ten could be carried.

The first Railway Air Service to the Island *(as distinct from the joint Southern Railway/Spartan route)* was inaugurated on the 30th July 1934 when the Dragon G-ACPY flown by Flt Lt J.H. Spender arrived at Cowes at 11.30, the flight having picked up several dignitaries at Bristol and Southampton. A luncheon and reception was held at the Gloster Hotel, Cowes, the guests including the Mayor of Southampton *(Cllr W.D. Buck)*, Wing Commander A.H. Measures *(Superintendent Railway Air Services)*, Mr J.B. Elliot *(Assistant Traffic Manager, Southern Railway)*, Mr G.E. Outon *(Public Relations, Great Western Railway)*, Mr C Grasemann *(Assistant Chief Manager, Public Relations and Advertising, Southern Railway)*, Mr J.L. Harrington *(Special Projects, Southern Railway)* and Capt Lynch-Blosse *(Chief Pilot Spartan Airlines)*.

The service operated twice daily except Sundays and the timings were:-

Dep Birmingham *(Castle Bromwich)*	09.35	14.15
Arr Bristol *(Whitchurch)*	10.30	15.10
Dep Bristol *(Whitchurch)*	10.35	15.15
Arr Southampton *(Eastleigh)*	11.15	15.55
Dep Southampton *(Eastleigh)*	11.20	16.00
Arr Cowes *(Somerton)*	11.30	16.10

The Liverpool - Birmingham service departed Liverpool at 08.45 connected with the 09.35 southbound departure from Birmingham, this flight also connected at Bristol with the Western Airways service from Cardiff and also to Bournemouth by the above airline.

Northbound the opposite applied and it should be noted that the total time from Liverpool to Cowes was 2 hours 45 minutes. Free surface transport was provided between the main stations in the above cities and their respective airports, this also applying at Cowes. A free baggage allowance of 35lbs was provided with an excess of up to 6d (2½p) per additional pound.

The fares were:-

	single	return
Cowes - Southampton	5/- (25p)	10/- (50p)
Cowes - Bristol	27/7 (£1.37p)	45/- (£2.25p)
Cowes - Birmingham	40/- (£2.00p)	72/6 (£3.63p)

The new service was also an advantage to Jersey Airways, which the railways would ultimately own, as it gave them onward connections to the Midlands and the North.

On July 24th the Postmaster General stated that the Post Office was considering using air services for the carriage of mail and an agreement was reached with Railway Air Services for such a service. If the letters weighed 2oz or less they were sent at the standard rate but above this the surcharge was one penny per extra ounce. The first mail was to be carried to the Island on August 20th but the weather was atrocious and Dragon G-ACPY on the Birmingham - Cowes route abandoned the attempt and terminated at Bristol, the mail being finally delivered the following day. The Dragon landed at Cowes at 11.45 and four bags of mail were unloaded. The reception committee consisted of the Mayor and Mayoress of Newport, the Mayor of Ryde, Mr C. Savage, the resident R.A.S. officer at Cowes,

BY AIR MAIL

COWES
INLAND AIR MAIL

Commencing on the 20th August, *Inland Air Mail Services* twice daily will be established on weekdays between Cowes and Birmingham, Bristol and Southampton at the following times :—

	p.m.	p.m.
Cowes (Somerton Aerodrome)	12. 5	5. 0
Southampton Airport	12.15	5.10
Bristol (Whitchurch Aerodrome)	1. 0	5.55
Birmingham (Castle Bromwich Aerodrome)	2. 0	6.55

The first service from Cowes to Birmingham will connect with the Air Mail Services to Belfast, Douglas (Isle of Man), Glasgow and Manchester, and the second Service with an Air Mail Service to Liverpool.

RATES OF POSTAGE

The *rates of postage* will be 1½d. for the first 2 oz. and 1d. for each subsequent ounce, for postcards 1d. each ; that is to say, there will be no increase in charge as compared with the ordinary service for letters not exceeding 2 oz. in weight, and for postcards.

USE OF AIR MAIL LABELS

All correspondence intended for despatch by Air Mail should bear a blue Air Mail label, and if one is not available, letters should be clearly endorsed " By Air Mail " on the left hand top corner of the envelope.

POSTINGS AND COLLECTIONS

The *latest times of posting* in Cowes for the places mentioned will be as follows :—

	a.m.	p.m.
Head Post Office	11. 0	4. 0
	8. 0	2. 0
General Collections from Street Letter Boxes between	and	and
	8.45	2.45

Mr W.K. Mackenzie *(Surveyor's Department G.P.O. Portsmouth),* Mr E.P. Robins of the Southern Railway, Mr J.H. Sender, the pilot, Mr A.J. Mew of the Isle of Wight Chamber of Commerce and Mr E.W. Stent, the local postman. After various speeches the Dragon departed at 12.20 with 2,500 items of mail.

From the 20th August, the Glasgow - London service connected with the Birmingham - Cowes route thus making it possible to fly from Glasgow to Cowes leaving Glasgow *(Renfrew)* at 9.15am, arriving in Birmingham at 12.40pm with the connecting Cowes aircraft leaving at 2.15pm arriving Cowes at 4.10pm. The Glasgow - Birmingham service called en route at Belfast and Manchester. The northbound service departed Cowes at 12.05 arriving Birmingham at 2.00pm. A passenger then had to wait until 4.05pm for the Glasgow departure which arrived at the latter at 7.30pm. There was also a late afternoon departure from Cowes to Birmingham via Southampton and Bristol with a connection to Liverpool.

As Railway Air Services were majority owned by the railways, the Airline had distinct advantages over other internal operators and particularly so in ticketing and marketing. In addition to booking at normal Airline offices potential passengers were able to make reservations at main line stations, this being later fully exploited by extending this facility to the vast majority of railway stations. Excess baggage *(over the 35lb free allowance)* could be sent by train direct to the passengers home or hotel. This scheme also applied to Spartan AirLines.

The route was normally worked by Dragon G-ACPY or G-ACPX but on occasions another aircraft was substituted and Dragon G-ACVD is known to have worked the Island route. On the 29th September the service was suspended for the winter and as the Dragons were chartered they were returned with G-ACPX going to de Havilland's and G-ACPY to Olley Air Services and thence to Western Airways. From the 1st to the 31st October Spartan Airlines operated

Railway Air Services Dragon ex 'City of Cardiff' renamed 'Island Maid' at Bournemouth   Credit: Maurice

Railway Air Services DH84 Dragon G-ADDI at Shoreham   Credit: Shoreham Airport Collection

on behalf of Railway Air Services and for the rest of the winter Spartan carried on alone, the route being:
 Bembridge - Cowes - Southampton *(not Sundays)* - Croydon.

1935

For the 1935 season Railway Air Services had at last taken delivery of two new de Havilland 89 Dragon Rapides. The impression is sometimes given that the Rapide was a "cleaned up" Dragon but in fact it was a completely new aircraft. As with the Dragon the design philosophy of economy of operation combined with minimum maintenance was rigidly applied. The Rapide was first flown on 17th April 1934 and like its predecessor was a two bay biplane but with wings that tapered almost to a point, a fully

Junkers 52/3M at Sandown, 1936   Credit: Henry Nobbs

the class of aeroplane which is rightly intended for reliable pilots". Reacting to this criticism de Havilland produced a version which was fitted with flaps and designated this the 89A. The flaps enabled steeper approaches to be made which in turn shortened the landing run to 170 yards from 220 yards. Operators took advantage of this and most of the original aircraft were retrofitted with flaps, the take off distance, fully loaded, for both versions being 290 yards.

enclosed trousered undercarriage and powered by two Gypsy Six engines each producing a maximum of 200hp which gave a cruising speed of 132mph. The Rapide was designed, like its predecessor, to carry eight passengers. In almost every respect the Rapide was an excellent aircraft but with a wing loading of only 14lbs/sq ft at maximum weight and no flaps there was a tendency to float and a number of pilots complained about this. "The Aeroplane" magazine remarked upon this by stating that "The Rapide was

In terms of numbers built the Rapide was the most successful of pre war British twin engine commercial aircraft with some 730 being produced. During World War II the RAF, the Fleet Air Arm and the Air Transport Auxiliary operated them under the name of Dominie. It was so successful that it was used post war by a number of operators and no replacement appeared until the the de Havilland Dove in 1945 and later the Britten Norman Islander in 1967.

Railway Air Services ordered a total of eight Rapides, the two which were allocated to the Island routes were G-ACPP "City of Bristol" and G-ACPR "City of Birmingham". Others identified as operating the route were G-AEAJ "Star of Lancashire" and G-AEAL "Star of Yorkshire".

The Island services re-started on the 25th May 1935 but with Portsmouth being substituted for Ryde, with two services per weekday (*no services on Sundays*) in both directions. The timings were revised and to prevent the Island being isolated a Sandown - Cowes - Southampton ferry was operated from the same date. There were six flights per weekday (*eight during the first week of August*) with some flights connecting with the Southampton - Bristol - Birmingham - Liverpool service. The service was worked by either Dragon G-ACNI or G-ACNG with 2481 passengers being carried by the ferry. The route was actually being flown by Spartan Airlines under charter to Railway Air Services.

Publicity drawing of Dragon Rapide
Credit: British Aerospace PLC

PASSENGERS LUGGAGE IN ADVANCE
CARRIAGE PAID

RAILWAY AIR SERVICES
LTD

LONDON AND
ISLE OF WIGHT SERVICE

IN CONJUNCTION WITH
SPARTAN AIR LINES LTD

By arrangement with CARTER PATERSON & Co Ltd

Railway Air Services Dragon Rapide G-ACPP 'City of Bristol'   Credit: Richard Riding

A passenger to Birmingham had the choice of two departures from Sandown, namely, at 09.10 and 4.40pm which connected at Southampton at 09.50 and 5.20pm respectively. The actual flying time between Sandown and Birmingham was 2 hours and 5 minutes and the fares were 43/- single *(£2.15)* and 77/6 return *(£3.87)*.

On the same date as the mainline route opened, a completely new route commenced being Sandown - Cowes - Southampton - Portsmouth - Shoreham and was worked on a twice daily basis except Sundays. Departures were from Sandown at 10.40 and 6.10pm arriving Shoreham at 11.50 and 7.20pm respectively. the aircraft that operated the latter arrival stayed overnight at Shoreham and then worked the 09.10 departure the following morning. The Sandown - Shoreham fare was 20/- *(£1.00)* single and 35/- *(£1.75)* return. Shoreham Airport served Worthing, Hove and Brighton and there was a Southern Railway station virtually on the Airport named "Bungalow Town Halt" but on the 3rd June 1935 was re-named Shoreham Airport. The train connections ensured that a passenger would be at Worthing station 18 minutes after arrival at Shoreham Airport, the corresponding figures for Hove and Brighton were 31 and 35 minutes respectively. One may ask why Railway Air Services did not operate an Island - London service but this was already catered for by their partners Spartan AirLines. Connections were also advertised to the Channel Islands, Cardiff, Newton Abbot, Teignmouth, Torquay, Plymouth, Nottingham, Blackpool and the Isle of Man. By closely studying the timetables of the various airlines that serviced the Island it was possible to travel to virtually every major centre in the country. As the Liverpool - Shoreham service only operated six days per week it meant that the aircraft would be idle at Shoreham on Sundays and in order to avoid this it was decided to operate a seasonal Sundays only Shoreham - le Touquet service.

At 19.05 on the 25th August the Dragon Rapide G-ACPP "City of Bristol" took off in poor visibility from le Touquet for its return to Shoreham. The occupants were the pilot, a married couple and one other passenger. Due to the poor visibility the pilot decided to fly along the French coast to Boulogne, cross the channel at its narrowest and mark the landfall at Dungeness, but unfortunately his compass and radio were unserviceable. To add to his troubles one engine started to run rough and having been airborne for 70 minutes a certain apprehension began to be felt, this feeling being enhanced by the pilot announcing he was completely lost but believed they were heading for Sweden! Some time later a passenger spotted a boat and the pilot ordered the passengers to prepare for ditching but fortunately just at

Dragon Rapide G-ACPP 'City of Bristol' after   Credit: Henry Nobbs
its extended flight from le Touquet 25th August 1935!

Interior of Dragon Rapide   Credit: British Aerospace PLC

Instrument panel of Dragon Rapide   Credit: British Aerospace PLC

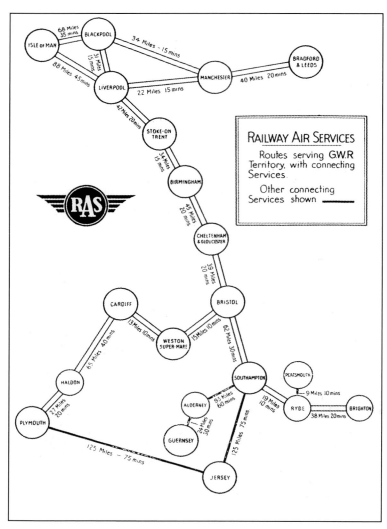

Schematic showing routes 1936

1936

Several changes occurred during the year, the mainline terminal now being Manchester instead of Liverpool. The most important changes as far as the Island was concerned was the transfer of the Island airport from Cowes to Ryde, which incidently was owned by rival PSIOWA. The reasons given were that Ryde had better terminal and handling facilities, but from the pilots' point of view Ryde was on higher ground and less subject to fog. Another reason was that Ryde was nearer the Island's east coast resorts such as Sandown, Shanklin and Ventnor and thus it became the Island's main airport and would remain so until the outbreak of war. Ryde was once again introduced on the direct mainline route thus saving Island passengers having to change at Southampton. Subject to 24 hours notice a request stop was introduced at Meir *(for Stoke-on-Trent)* and from June a similar arrangement applied at Staverton *(for Cheltenham and Gloucester)* with only three hours prior notice being required. They were two departures per day from Ryde on Mondays, Tuesdays, Fridays and Saturdays at 10.05am and 5.05pm, the latter terminating at Liverpool. On the other weekdays the morning departure was deleted. A new Sundays only service was introduced from the 5th July to the 6th September which departed Ryde at 6.10 for Southampton - Bristol - Weston-Super-Mare - Cardiff. Railway Air Services also operated a joint service with Spartan AirLines from and to Gatwick from Ryde and Cowes, details of which are given in the Chapter on Spartan Airlines.

that moment the same passenger spotted a lighthouse and shortly after the aircraft landed and nosed over just south of New Barn Farm, near Shanklin, Isle of Wight, the total flight time being 2.05 hours. The outcome of this episode was that the passengers sued Railway Air Services on the grounds that on take off the pilot was drunk, the aircraft was poorly maintained with faulty radio and compass plus the engine vibration was caused by an out of balance propeller. Railway Air Services settled paying £4,250 plus £1,000 costs between the plaintiffs, the pilot's employment being terminated. To put this settlement into perspective the average male earnings in 1935 was £148 per annum. The aircraft was repaired and served with various owners and was exported to Canada in 1961. From the 16th September the winter schedules came into effect and all services operated on a reduced basis.

Another innovation was the introduction of a direct local service between Ryde and Shoreham with two departures per day, except for Wednesdays and Thursdays. This was supplemented from the 5th July by an additional departure from Ryde at 11.20am. The flight time was 20 minutes. The standard return fare was 24/- *(£1.20)* but on weekdays there was a day excursion fare of 15/- *(75p).*

As in the previous year, the Ryde - Liverpool - Manchester route was now flown by the two Dragon Rapides G-ACPP 'City of Bristol' and G-ACPR 'City of Birmingham', the latter aircraft also being used to convert Imperial Airways pilots to Railway Air Services routes. It is believed that the Dragon G-ADDJ 'City of Plymouth' was used on the direct Ryde - Shoreham service, but it may well have also been used on the Gatwick - Ryde to supplement its RAS/Spartan stablemate G-ACNI.

The total number of passengers carried by Railway Air Services during 1936 was 22,103.

1937

The Spring schedule started in March but as far as it can be ascertained, operations were as in 1936 with the summer schedule Liverpool - Manchester - Birmingham - Bristol - Southampton - Ryde - Shoreham commencing on the 10th May. The timings were believed to be identical to the previous year. Aircraft that worked the route were once again Dragon Rapides G-ACPP and G-ACPR.

1938

As in 1937 it would appear that the company policy was one of consolidation. This involved experiments with timings and frequencies as this affected the traffic returns and obviously the intention was to maximise this factor. A new route came into existence during the year which was Shoreham - Ryde - Bournemouth. Part of this route was already being operated by Portsmouth, Southsea and Isle of Wight Aviation Ltd, and in order to avoid uneconomical competition, a pooling of receipts was agreed between the companies. On this route P.S.I.O.W.A. operated the R.A.S. Dragon G-ADDI 'Island Maid', previously 'City of Cardiff'. In September 1938 this aircraft was transferred to Channel Air Ferries who was used it on the Lands End (*St Just*) -

Scilly Isles route. On the 17th December 1938 it failed to become airborne and was badly damaged in the resultant crash. It must have been re-built quickly as it was operating in 1939 and was still flying in the United States in 1996!

During the year and in order to reflect more accurately the various railway companies territorial interests, a major re-organisation was put into effect whereby a new company was formed and known as Great Western and Southern Airlines Ltd. An agreement was reached with British and Foreign Aviation Ltd and the two railways, shares being allocated on the basis of 25% each for the railways and 50% for British and Foreign Aviation Ltd. This company, through Olley Air Services Ltd, owned Channel Air Ferries and with the exception of Portsmouth,

Bar at Croydon

Credit: Science Museum/Science & Society Library

Railway Air Services check in at Croydon   Credit: Science Museum/Science & Society Library

Southsea and Isle of Wight Aviation Ltd eliminated virtually all competition on the Island routes. Great Western and Southern Railways Airlines did not actually come into being until March 1939, but on the 1st August 1938 a management team was set up to amalgamate the companies. The base was to be at Shoreham and Gordon Olley was appointed Managing Director. Between August 1938 and March 1939 R.A.S. and C.A.F. operated under their own names, but from March onward the existing names were dropped and all operations were under the title of Great Western and Southern Airlines Ltd. With this action R.A.S. dropped out of the Isle of Wight routes and concentrated on routes to the North.

At its peak in 1937, R.A.S. carried some 25,523 passengers and flew some 1,004,196 miles but unfortunately, it has not been possible to isolate the passenger figures for the Isle of Wight routes. When the Maybury Committee reported in December 1936 it was very critical of the conduct of the Railways and of R.A.S., the criticism being levelled at their predatory practices. Their losses were £14,541 in 1934, £43,196 in 1935, £51,468 in 1937 and in 1938 a somewhat smaller loss than in the previous year of £42,000. The Committee took grave exception to the fact that independent travel agents who booked passengers with other airlines, apart from Imperial Airways, were banned by the Railways, this applying to both air and rail travel. The ruling came into

Railway Air Services Dragon Rapide G-ACPR 'City of Birmingham' at Ryde. The figure by the starboard engine is Howard Shaw, the airport's accredited taxi driver.

Railway Air Services Dragon Rapide 'Star of Scotia'

Credit: Mike Hooks

Railway Air Services Fleet

Credit: Science Museum/Science & Society Library

being in 1933 and had the effect of forcing would be passengers to book either at the Railway Stations or through the Railways tied travel agents. This scheme carried through to 1938 and was only dropped when the Government threatened action. With regard to the R.A.S. losses the Railway showed little inclination to organise themselves efficiently preferring to adopt the longer term practice of forcing their competitors out of business and thus limiting competition.

In 1944 the Railway Companies Association produced a plan for post War participation in air services involving a massive expansion involving both internal and continental routes and to fly some 20 million miles in the first year. In discussions with the Government they undertook to operate without any subsidies and now viewed the air as a primary means of

transport. They were prepared to offer partnerships with other operators. Sir Harold Hartley of Railway Air Services and Mr L.M.J. Balfour of Portsmouth Aviation Ltd had a series of meetings which culminated in formal approval of the proposed scheme by Lord Swinton, the Air Minister in the Churchill Government. It was agreed between the two companies that they would join forces and to expand Ryde airport, already owned by PSIOWA, into a regional hub offering the latest navigational aids, customs and immigration. This would have brought significant employment benefits to the area but it was not to be as the Labour Government of 1945 decreed that only a State Corporation would be allowed to operate scheduled services, so once again the dead hand of bureaucracy stifled private enterprise and potential prosperity.

Aircraft of Railway Air Services & their Ultimate Fate

(Refers only to aircraft used on the Isle of Wight services)

DE HAVILLAND 84 DRAGONS

G-ACNI (6971)
Used during 1936 season on the R.A.S./ Spartan Gatwick - Island schedule. Believed to have been sold to Irish Air Corp. in 1937.

G-ACPX (6075)
Delivered May 1934. Worked Birmingham - Cowes route. Transferred to Western Airways. Impressed by RAF April 1940. Believed scrapped.

G-ACVD (6084)
Delivered 24th July 1934. Worked Birmingham - Cowes service. This aircraft was re-registered in 1937 as VH-UZX *(an Australian registration)* but strangely it was recorded as crashing at Beddington, Surrey on 26th February 1938.

G-ADDI (6096)
Delivered May 1935. Railway Air Services as 'City of Cardiff'. The name was changed to 'Island Maid' when it operated the Shoreham - Ryde - Bournemouth and then the Shoreham - Ryde - Manchester services. In September 1938 it was transferred to Channel Air Ferries and then Great Western and Southern Airlines. Under this ownership it operated the Scilly Islands - Penzance route. Various post war operators until February 1961 when it was sold in the USA as N34DH. Believed to be still flying in 1996.

G-ADDJ (6097)
'City of Plymouth' - delivered May 1935. In winter of 1936/1937 it operated on behalf of Railway Air Services on its South coast and Isle of Wight routes by Portsmouth, Southsea and Isle of Wight Aviation. Sold to Australia in march 1937 and registered as VH-UZZ. Impressed into RAAF in January 1940. Fate not known.

DE HAVILLAND 89 DRAGON RAPIDES

G-ACPP (6254)
'City of Bristol' - Delivered March 1935. Worked the Liverpool - Isle of Wight - Shoreham route. Transferred to Great Western and Southern Airlines in 1939. Continued to work the Island routes up to the start of hostilities on 3rd September 1939. Taken over by British European Airways. Sold to Canada as CF-PTK in June 1961. Fate not known.

G-ACPR (6255)
Delivered March 1935. Worked the Liverpool - Isle of Wight - Shoreham route. Transferred to Great Western and Southern Airlines in 1939. Continued to work the Island routes up to the outbreak of war. Written off 19th February 1940.

G-AEAJ (6320)
Delivered 14th March 1936 and named 'Star of Lancashire'. In October 1937 transferred to Isle of Man Air Services. Impressed January 1940.

G-AEAL (6325)
Delivered 25th April 1936, named "Star of Yorkshire". Transferred to Isle of Man Air Services in October 1937. Used post war by Hunting Aerosurveys and Wolverhampton Aviation and subsequently sold in the Ivory Coast as F-OAUE in April 1956. Fate unknown.

Railway Air Services Aircraft Specifications

de HAVILLAND DRAGON II

Power Plant	2 x 130HP Gipsy Majors
Wingspan	47' 4"
Length	34 '6"
Max all up weight	4,500lbs
Max speed	134MPH
Cruising speed	114MPH
Range	545 miles
Accommodation	Up to 10 passengers on short routes

de HAVILLAND DRAGON RAPIDE

Power Plant	2 x 200HP Gipsy Six
Wingspan	48' 0"
Length	34 '6"
Max all up weight	5,500lbs
Max speed	157MPH
Cruising speed	132MPH
Range	578 miles
Accommodation	Up to 10 passengers on short routes

Railway Air Services Ltd possessed other types but only those that worked the Isle of Wight routes are shown.

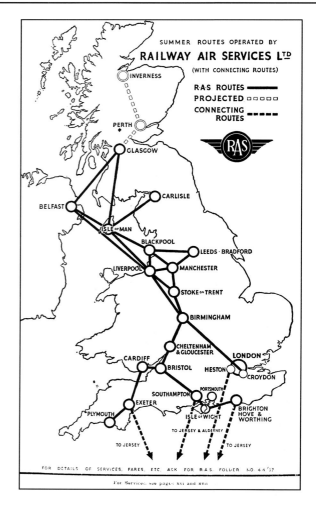

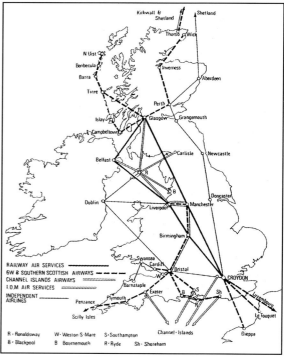

Railway Associated Airlines 1939
Credit: Science Museum/Science & Society Library

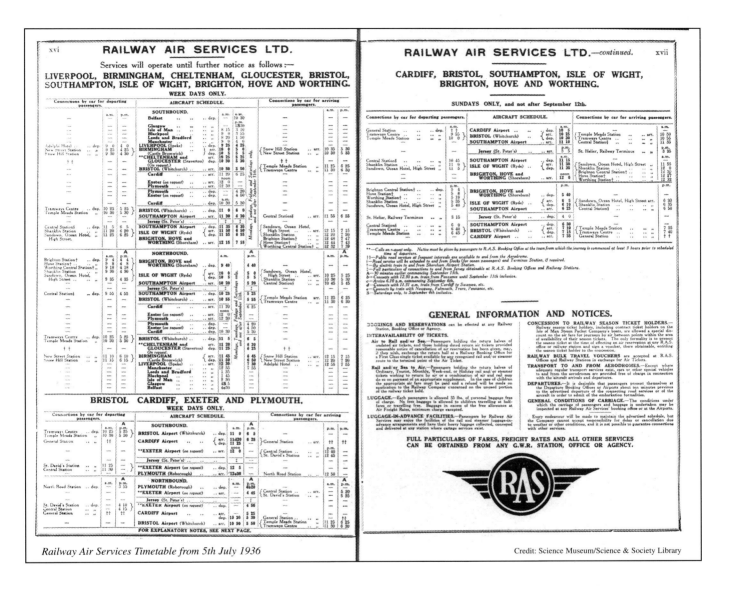

Railway Air Services Timetable from 5th July 1936

Credit: Science Museum/Science & Society Library

TABLE No. 7.

MANCHESTER, LIVERPOOL, BIRMINGHAM, GLOUCESTER, BRISTOL, SOUTHAMPTON, ISLE OF WIGHT, BRIGHTON, HOVE and WORTHING

WEEK-DAYS ONLY.

For increased service BRIGHTON & ISLE OF WIGHT beginning July 5th, see Table No. 10.

For Sunday Service BRISTOL, SOUTHAMPTON, ISLE OF WIGHT and BRIGHTON, see Table No. 9.

SOUTHBOUND.

Connections by car for departing passengers.	a.m.	p.m.	AIRCRAFT SCHEDULE.		a.m.	a.m.	Connections by car for arriving passengers.	a.m.	p.m.
			Belfast ... ... dep.			10.30	See Tables Nos. 2 and 3.		
					a.m.	p.m.			
			Isle of Man ... ,,		8.15	3.30			
			Blackpool ... ,,		9. 0	3.45			
London Road Station ... dep.	8.15	3.15	Leeds & Bradford ,,		8.30				
Parker Street Bus Station ,,	8.20	3.20	MANCHESTER (Barton) dep.		9. 0	4.10			
Midland Hotel ... ,,	8.25	3.25	LIVERPOOL (Speke) arr.		9.15	4.25			
Victoria Station ... ,,	8.30	3.30	dep.		9.25	4.30	Adelphi Hotel ... ... arr.	9.45	4.50
Adelphi Hotel ... ,,	8.55	4. 5	‡STOKE-ON-TRENT				††		
			(Meir) (*On request*) ... arr.		9.40	4.45			
			dep.		9.45	4.50			
Snow Hill Station ... ,,	9.30	4.35	BIRMINGHAM (Castle						
New Street Station ... ,,	9.35	4.40	Bromwich) ... arr.		10. 0	5. 5	New Street Station ... ,,	10.25	5.30
			dep.		10. 5	5.10	Snow Hill Station ... ,,	10.35	5.35
††			§CHELTENHAM and				††		
			GLOUCESTER						
			(Staverton) (*On request*) arr.		10.25	5.25			
Tramways Centre ... ,,	10.25	5.25	dep.		10.30	5.30	Temple Meads Station ,,	11.25	6.25
Temple Meads Station ,,	10.30	5.30	BRISTOL (Whitchurch) arr.		10a50	5d50	Tramways Centre ... ,,	11.30	6.30
			dep.		11b 0	6e 5			
Central Station* * ... ,,	11. 5	6.10	SOUTHAMPTON AIR-				Central Station* * ... ,,	12. 0	7. 0
			PORT ... arr.		11c30	6.35			
			dep.		11.40	6.40	Sandown, Ocean Hotel,		
Shanklin Station ... ,,	11.15	6.15	ISLE OF WIGHT (Ryde) arr.		11.50	6.50	High Street	12.10	7.10
Sandown, Ocean Hotel,			dep.		11.55	6.55	Shanklin Station ... ,,	12.20	7.20
High Street	11.20	6.20	BRIGHTON, HOVE &				Brighton Central Station†	12.47	7.47
			WORTHING (Shore-				Hove Station†	12.42	7.42
			ham) ... arr.		12.15	7.15	Worthing Station†	12.32	7.35

Mondays, Tuesdays, Fridays and Saturdays only.

NORTHBOUND

Connections by car for departing passengers.	a.m.	p.m.	AIRCRAFT SCHEDULE.		a.m.	p.m.	Connections by car for arriving passengers.	a.m.	p.m.
Brighton Central Station† dep.	9. 4	4. 4	BRIGHTON, HOVE &						
Hove Station† ... ,,	9. 8	4. 8	WORTHING (Shore-						
Worthing Station† ... ,,	9.18	4.18	ham) ... dep.		9.40	4.40			
Shanklin Station ... ,,	9.30	4.30	ISLE OF WIGHT (Ryde) arr.		10. 0	5. 0	Sandown, Ocean Hotel,		
Sandown, Ocean Hotel,			dep.		10. 5	5. 5	High Street arr.	10.20	5 20
High Street ,,	9.35	4.35	SOUTHAMPTON AIR-				Shanklin Station ... ,,	10.30	5.30
Central Station* * ... ,,	9.50	4.50	PORT ... arr.		10c15	5.15			
			dep.		10. 25	5g25	Central Station* * ... ,,	10.45	5.45
Tramways Centre ... ,,	10.25	5.25	BRISTOL (Whitchurch) arr.		10a55	5d55	Temple Meads Station ,,	11.25	6.25
Temple Meads Station ,,	10.30	5.30	dep.		11b 5	6e 5	Tramways Centre ... ,,	11.30	6.30
††			§CHELTENHAM and				††		
			GLOUCESTER						
			(Staverton) (*On request*) arr.		11.20	6.20			
			dep.		11.25	6.25			
Snow Hill Station ... ,,	11.15	6.15	BIRMINGHAM (Castle				New Street Station ... ,,	12.10	7.10
New Street Station ... ,,	11.20	6.20	Bromwich) ... arr.		11.45	6.45	Snow Hill Station ... ,,	12.15	7.15
			dep.		11.50	6.50			
††			‡STOKE-ON-TRENT				††		
			(Meir) (*On request*) ... arr.		12. 5	7. 5			
			dep.		12.10	7.10			
Adelphi Hotel ... ,,	12. 0	7.40	LIVERPOOL (Speke) arr.		12.30	7.30	Adelphi Hotel ... ,,	1. 5	7.55
			dep.		12.35	*8.10	Victoria Station ... ,,	1.20	8.55
			MANCHESTER (Barton) arr.		12.50	*8.25	Midland Hotel ... ,,	1.25	9. 0
			Leeds & Bradford ,,		1.10		Parker Street Bus Station ... ,,	1.30	9. 5
			Blackpool ... ,, arr.		2.15		London Road Station ... ,,	1.35	9.10
			Isle of Man ... ,,		3. 0				
See Tables Nos. 2 and 3.			Belfast ... ... ,,		6.30				

Mondays, Tuesdays, Fridays and Saturdays only.

See Tables Nos. 2 and 3

NOTES.— a—Connects to Weston-super-Mare, Cardiff, Torquay, Teignmouth, Newton Abbot and Plymouth (see Table No. 8). b—Connection from Cardiff and Weston-super-Mare (see Table No. 8). c—Connects to Alderney and Guernsey, Wednesdays excepted, and on most days to Jersey. d—Connects to Weston-super-Mare and Cardiff (see Table No. 8). e—Connection from Plymouth, Torquay, Teignmouth, Newton Abbot, Cardiff and Weston-super-Mare (see Table No. 8). g—Connection from Guernsey and Alderney (Wednesdays excepted) and on most days from Jersey.
* 30 minutes earlier commencing September 7th.   † By Electric train to and from Shoreham Airport Station.
‡ Calls on request at Stoke on 24 hours' notice being given to any R.A.S. Booking Office.
§ Calls on request at Cheltenham and Gloucester, commencing about June 20th. Notice must be given by passengers to R.A.S. Booking Office at the town from which the journey is commenced at least 3 hours prior to Scheduled time of departure.
†† Public road services at frequent intervals are available to and from the Aerodromes at Cheltenham, Gloucester and Stoke-on-Trent.
** Road service will be extended to and from Docks (for ocean passengers) and Terminus Station, if required.

Railway Air Services Timetable 25th May 1936

Credit: Science Museum/Science & Society Library

Channel Air Ferries Ltd & Great Western & Southern Airlines Ltd

Short Scion II G-ADDO of Channel Air Ferries

Credit: Shoreham Airport Collection

Captain Gordon Olley, the founder of Channel Air Ferries, was a well known character in the pioneering airline scene. In August 1914 he joined the Queen Victoria Rifles and on the first parade, before being attested, and still in civilian clothes, he objected to the Drill Sergeant standing on his feet and promptly hit him! He thus departed the scene but immediately enlisted in the Royal Fusiliers as a Dispatch Rider and sent to France. He later persuaded his Commanding Officer to recommend him for flying duties and remustered as a Corporal Observer serving with No 1 Squadron. Later in the war there was an acute shortage of pilots and once again Olley was successful. He went solo after three hours and upon completion of his training was posted to his old squadron as a Sergeant Pilot. During his service with this unit he shot down thirteen enemy aircraft and was awarded the Military Medal. In 1917 he was posted back to England and became a Ferry Pilot delivering aircraft to France, continuing in this duty until the cessation of hostilities. His first post war job was working for Handley Page flying their converted 0/400 bombers from Cricklewood to Paris and Brussels. this coming to an end

when all British airlines flying to the Continent ceased operation as due to lack of Government aid they could not compete with the heavily subsidised French airlines. For the next few weeks Olley worked for the Dutch airline KLM but in the meantime the British airlines and the Government had reached an agreement for a subsidy on Continental routes. Internal airlines were not included in this scheme and no subsidies for these services were to be granted until 1939. Olley returned to Handley Page and stayed with them until the formation of Imperial Airways in March 1924 when he and a number of other pilots transferred. Flying to a timetable was not really a practical proposition in those days and this is amply illustrated by Olley's experience on one London - Paris flight where, due to faulty fuel feed, he had to land a total of seventeen times and hand pump petrol from one tank to another.

After a period of two years with Imperial Airways he was appointed Charter Manager but this could not have occupied his time fully as he continued route flying and in 1928 was the pilot in what may be politely called a Public Relations

Dragon G-ADDI ex 'City of Cardiff' and 'Island Maid'
after failure to become airborne at St Just, Lands End 17.12.38 (Capt Lazella),
it was later repaired and was still flying in the USA in 1996.

Credit: Morrab Library, Penzance

Exercise. The event which took place on June 15th was to be a race between the crack train the 'Flying Scotsman' and an Armstrong Whitworth Argosy G-EBLF 'City of Glasgow' of Imperial Airways. The train and the aircraft were to leave London at precisely the same time and the first to reach Edinburgh station would be the winner. The 'Flying Scotsman' was able to travel non stop but Olley would have to land twice to refuel and to ensure fair play an engine driver flew with Olley and a pilot travelled on the footplate of the locomotive, journalists accompanying both forms of transport. Olley's aim was to fly over the Royal Border Bridge where photographers would be waiting but when overhead he unfortunately picked the wrong train which was running five minutes behind the 'Flying Scotsman', the engine driver accompanying Olley only realising this when the train stopped at a station. Olley accordingly increased speed and arrived 15 minutes ahead of the train, but by the time he and his passengers arrived at Edinburgh's Waverley station the occupants of the train were waiting for them on the concourse.

As charter manager Olley was responsible for organising the chartering of aircraft to influential personalities one of which was a Captain Loewenstein, a long standing customer. Loewenstein was a multi millionaire Belgian financier who permanently chartered eight aircraft from Imperial and which were based at his home in Biarritz. Olley was deputed as operations manager being provided with a villa complete with a valet and a chauffeur. Loewenstein was an individual of tremendous energy and would think nothing of summoning Olley in the middle of the night to fly him and

his staff to some destination or other but in due course of time such pressure affected Loewenstein's health and with it his business acumen. By 1928 the chartering had been reduced to one aircraft namely Fokker VIII/3M G-EBYI *(ex KLM)*. On the 4th July he chartered this aircraft to take him from Croydon to Brussels but over the Channel it was discovered that the main door was open and no trace of Loewenstein could be found. He certainly had business worries and several writers have propounded theories, including that he mistook the exit door for the toilet, but this was unlikely as he was an experienced traveller. Whether it was suicide or accident has never been established but this incident may well have been the inspiration for the novel 'Murder in the Air' by Agatha Christie.

Later Olley decided to form his own company and obtained the backing of Sir Hugo Cunliffe-Owen, the Chairman of British American Tobacco Company. Olley Air Services Ltd was formed on the 10th January 1934 with a capital of £6,015 and immediately started charter operations from Croydon using two new de Havilland Dragons G-ACPY and G-ACNA. The company must have been successful as a year later he formed Isle of Man Air Services Ltd and shortly after took over Blackpool and West Coast Air Services Ltd. Not a man to stand still, in August 1935 he acquired the assets of Cobham Air Services which flew between Croydon - Portsmouth - Bournemouth and Guernsey. On the 8th May 1936 he formed Channel Air Ferries and commencing on the 23rd of the same month he offered a service between Shoreham and Ryde on a daily basis in both directions. The policy of Channel Air Ferries was not to purchase aircraft

Great Western & Southern Airlines Dragon Rapide at Shoreham

but to arrange inter company transfers as required. The only exception to this was the Short Scion II G-ADDO which was in fact the personal property of the Earl of Amhurst, a director. This aircraft has been identified as operational on the Shoreham - Ryde route. When the service finished for the season in September 453 passengers had been carried.

Channel Air Ferries made Shoreham their base and were awarded the contract to manage the airport on the 3rd June 1935. The Southern Railway Station on the airport boundary which was called Bungalow Town Halt was re-named Shoreham Airport (for Brighton, Hove and Worthing).

1937

From the 1st July Channel Air Ferries commenced a Shoreham - Bembridge - Ryde service and one week later extended this to Bournemouth, from which Bournemouth there were connections via Western Airways to Bristol and Cardiff. September must have been a popular month as all South Coast and I.O.W. airlines reported record figures and on the 11th Channel Air Ferries manager at Shoreham had to turn away passengers. On 15th September 1937 and, in addition to the Isle of Wight services, C.A.F. opened another over water route this time from Land's End (St Just) to the Scilly Isles. The route became very successful and in 1938 it operated at three return flights per day carrying some 5,000 passengers in it's first year, thus making it possible to fly from Bembridge to the Scillies via Bournemouth - Bristol - Cardiff - Exeter and Plymouth. In order to co-ordinate his various interests Olley formed a holding company named

British and foreign Aviation Ltd, the shares of his various companies being held by this body. To supplement the schedules Olley was very active in charters and was the major operator in race meeting charters which covered all the important race meetings in the country.

1938

By now C.A.F. considerably expanded its route structure and on the 21st February inaugurated a Heston - Croydon - Shoreham - Bembridge - Bournemouth - Bristol - Cardiff service as follows:-

Depart	Cardiff	13.40
	Bristol	15.00
	Bournemouth	15.40
	Bembridge	16.05
	Shoreham	16.40
	Croydon	17.10
Arrive	Heston	17.20
Depart	Heston	10.40
	Croydon	11.00
	Shoreham	11.35
	Bembridge	12.05
	Bournemouth	12.30
	Bristol	13.10
Arrive	Cardiff	13.25

During Easter and Summer peak periods additional services were offered including a direct Heston - Bembridge service which operated once a day on Thursdays, Fridays and Saturdays leaving Heston at 10.00 and Bembridge at 11.00 with the flight time of 30 minutes. In order to cater for returning holiday-makers on Sundays and Mondays the flights departed Bembridge for Heston at 15.30 and 17.30 respectively. The timetable indicated that there were also connections to Dublin and the continent.

The fare from Heston to Bembridge was 29/- *(£1.45)* single and 46/- *(£2.30)* return.

During 1938 Gordon Olley was awarded the prestigious GAPAN Trophy (Guild of Air Pilots and Navigators - a City Livery Company) for his contribution to air safety and reliability. As stated in the chapter on Railway Air Services, in 1938 the Railway Companies decided to rationalise their investment and as the Great Western and Southern Railways interests were in the South and West they decided to form a new company named Great Western and Southern Airlines, the other shareholder being British and Foreign Aviation Ltd; Olley's holding company.

The shareholding was 25% each for the Great Western and Southern Railways and the remaining 50% by British and Foreign Aviation Ltd, the company being incorporated on 5th December with a capital of £100,000. The Directors were J.O.H. Elliot *(later Sir)*, K.W.C. Grand and Wing Commander A.H. Measures, all representing the railways and Gordon Olley (Managing), J.W.S. Comber and J.S. Wills representing British and Foreign Aviation Ltd. The Company's base was Shoreham and the Earl of Amhurst M.C. was appointed General Manager. The Chief Pilot was J.H. Nicholas and H.P. Snelling became the Traffic Manager. Before the actual incorporation a Management Committee was set up to amalgamate the activities of both companies and this committee remained until the merger was completed on the 24th March 1939. Until that date the companies traded under their individual names but upon the merger becoming effective the name Channel Air Ferries disappeared and consequently all services were under the name of Great Western and Southern Airlines.

Contemporaneously with these happenings the Government established the Air Transport Licencing Authority and all airlines had to apply for licences to operate. The area allocated on the 21st October 1938 to Great Western and Southern Airlines was in effect the old Railway Air Services Isle of Wight routes from Manchester through to Shoreham and Channel Air Ferries Shoreham - Bembridge - Bournemouth, Bristol - Cardiff, Plymouth - Land's End, Scilly Isles. They were also granted the authority to continue to operate the C.A.F. direct Heston - Bembridge service.

On the 3rd April 1939 Great Western and Southern Airlines began their local Shoreham - Isle of Wight - Bournemouth

service and the receipts pooling arrangement with PSIOWA on the Island - Bournemouth sector continued. At the beginning of the season the Island stop was transferred from Bembridge to Ryde. This airfield possessed better handling facilities and was more convenient for passengers whose destinations were Portsmouth or Southampton (with connections to the Channel Islands) and therefore would be able to transfer at Ryde straight onto the PSIOWA services to these points.

The fleet consisted of the following:-

From Railway Air Services
de Havilland 84 Dragon G-ADDI
de Havilland 89 Dragon Rapide G-ACPP
de Havilland 89 Dragon Rapide G-ACPR

From Channel Air Ferries
de Havilland 89 Dragon Rapide G-ACYM
de Havilland 84 Dragon G-ACPY
Short Scion G-ADDO
de Havilland Fox Moth G-ACFC
de Havilland Fox Moth G-ACFF

The Island was well served by Great Western and Southern Airlines and associated companies, examples of destinations that were available from Ryde were:-

Ryde - Bournemouth - Bristol - Exeter - Plymouth - Land's End - Scilly Isles

Ryde - Shoreham - Croydon
(for connections to the Continent and the Empire routes)

Ryde - Bournemouth - Bristol - Dublin

Ryde - Shoreham - Deauville

Ryde - Shoreham - Le Touquet

Ryde - Southampton - Bristol - Birmingham - Liverpool - Isle of Man
(onward connections were available by Railway Air Services and others to Belfast - Glasgow - Perth - Inverness - Wick - Kirkwall and Lerwick).

After the commencement of the local route on the 3rd April 1939 the next route to be opened on the 1st May was the old Railway Air Services route from Liverpool to Ryde and Shoreham and a few days later on the 7th a Cardiff - Bristol - Bournemouth - Ryde - Shoreham route was inaugurated. Finally on the 26th May a four times a week Heston - Croydon - Ryde service was introduced. In the short time up to the outbreak of War Great Western and Southern Airlines

CHANNEL AIR FERRIES, LTD.

Brighton, Isle of Wight, Bournemouth, Bristol, and Cardiff.

DAILY, EXCEPT TUESDAYS.

			A	
Brighton (Shoreham)	dep.	8 30	1 45	4 0
Isle of Wight (Bembridge)	arr.	8 55	2 10	4 25
Isle of Wight (Bembridge)	dep.	9 5	2 20	4 35
Bournemouth (Christchurch)	arr.	9 20	2 35	4 50
Bournemouth (Christchurch)	dep.	9 30	—	5 0
Bristol (Whitchurch)	arr.	10 0	—	5 30
Bristol (Whitchurch)	dep.	1010	—	5 40
Cardiff	arr.	1025	—	5 55

			A	•
Cardiff	dep.	1040	—	6 0
Bristol (Whitchurch)	arr.	1055	—	6 15
Bristol (Whitchurch)	dep.	11 5	—	6 25
Bournemouth (Christchurch)	arr.	1135	—	6 55
Bournemouth (Christchurch)	dep.	1145	2 50	7 5
Isle of Wight (Bembridge)	arr.	12 0	3 5	7 20
Isle of Wight (Bembridge)	dep.	1210	3 15	7 30
Brighton (Shoreham)	arr.	1230	3 35	7 50

A Commences 4th June.
• By Request.

1938 Timetable

carried 12,122 passengers and flew 261,000 miles.

On the 3rd September 1939 the the Air Navigation *(Restriction in Time of War)* Act was implemented and all civil flying to the Isle of Wight ceased. Great Western and Southern Airlines became part of the Associated Airlines Joint Committee *(A.A.J.C.)* which was formed by the Government to co-ordinate essential air transport services.

It was common practice to switch aircraft between routes and in 1939 the veteran Dragon G-ACPY which had worked the Island routes since 1934 was transferred to the Scilly Isles route. During the war the Scilly Isles route was kept open as an essential service and on the afternoon of 3rd June 1941 G-ACPY departed Scilly for its regular run to Lands End with five passengers but failed to arrive, it being assumed it had been shot down by either a Junkers 88 or an Arado 196, which was a reasonable assessment. According to an article by Mike Ingham in 'Air Enthusiast' No 66. It subsequently transpired that the Germans also could not identify the aircraft they had destroyed and therefore both sides were left in ignorance and the situation remained a mystery for over fifty years until a Herr Klenck made enquiries at the R.A.F. museum. This gentleman was at the time of the incident the Captain of a Heinkel III H-4 *(he was a Naval Officer and the navigator)* detailed to carry out a daylight bombing attack on the aircraft carrier H.M.S. Indomitable which was fitting out at Barrow-in-Furness, but when abeam the Pembroke coast the cloud cover disappeared leaving a clear sky and therefore it was decided

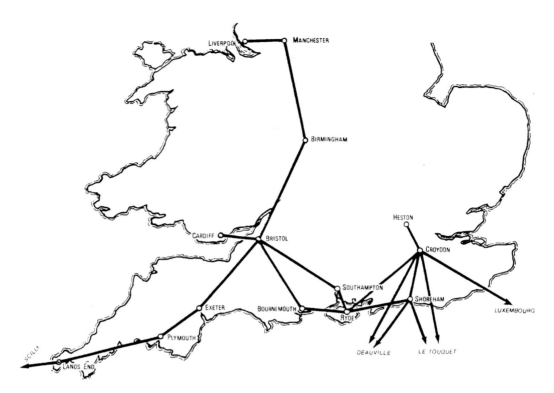

Great Western & Southern Airlines Routes 1939

to abort the mission. On the return leg they flew back into the overcast and were looking for the Scilly turning point when they saw the Dragon and attacked thus shooting it down, all aboard being killed. It must be considered that the Dragon being camouflaged was a legitimate target, but nevertheless and against orders the Heinkel crew put out a broadcast in the clear on the International Distress Frequency. It was ironic that until three days prior to the loss of the Dragon, a detachment of Hurricanes of 87 Squadron used the Scilly Isles as a forward base but were withdrawn on the 31st May.

Anticipating post-war expansion the L.M.S., G.W.R and S.R. acquired the entire share capital of British and Foreign Aviation thus making Great Western and Southern Airlines a wholly owned subsidiary of those railways but retaining Olley as Managing Director. In 1946 Olley Air Services recommenced operations with charters and in this field he was very active. After the 1st February 1947 no independent

airlines were allowed to operate scheduled services but in 1948 Olley signed a B.E.A. Associate agreement which allowed him to operate to schedules to Deauville and le Touquet. In 1951 this agreement was extended to include Croydon - Bristol - Weston-Super-Mare - Exeter - Newquay - Land's End. The following year he obtained a licence to operate to the Channel Islands. In 1953, the railways having been frustrated by the Government in their plans for comprehensive air services sold their interest in British and Foreign Aviation Ltd to Morton Air Services. Olley was retained as Managing Director but was not happy in this situation and resigned shortly after.

Olley was one of the outstanding pioneers of British civil aviation and had flown over 13,500 hours without injury to any passenger. He died on the 18th March 1958 aged 64. His ashes were scattered over Croydon Airport and he is commemorated by a road near the now defunct Croydon Airport appropriately named "Olley Close".

GW & SR Timetable 1939

Airports of the Isle of Wight & South Coast

Spartan's Terminal building - Bembridge 1935

Credit: Millichap/Croydon Airport Society

Bembridge

Bembridge has a long history of aviation, the first recorded activity that the author has traced is that of a Bleriot Monoplane outside the Royal Spithead Hotel in about 1911/12. It has not been possible to either establish the exact date or the purpose of the visit but the Bleriot appeared to be guarded by personnel from the nearby Coastguard Station. It should be noted that in those days the Coastguard wore uniforms similar to that of Naval ratings. one of the Officers at the R.N. College, Osborne owned a Bleriot but whether this is the same machine has not been established.

In 1915 the Admiralty was concerned that enemy submarines would operate in the vicinity of the Island and, in particular, to the approaches to Portsmouth Harbour and established a

Bembridge ex seaplane hanger in use as a theatre on Shanklin Seafront

Credit: The late Alan Parker

seaplane base at Bembridge Point. Initially this was intended to be of a temporary nature but in 1916 it was decided to permanently base four Short 184 Seaplanes and a hanger was built to accommodate them, the Officers living in the adjoining Royal Spithead Hotel and the ratings being billeted in a Coastguard Station. The Short 184's had the ability to patrol up to 60 miles from the Island and on the 18th October 1917 Flight Commander McLaurin and his observer spotted a surfaced U-Boat, immediately attacked and scored a direct hit with a 45kg bomb, the submarine was seen to submerge with a list of 30 degrees but the kill was not confirmed. The unit operated as 412 and 413 flights but were absorbed into 253 Squadron in August 1918, the establishment having at that time risen to 12 seaplanes and 190 officers and men. The Squadron was disbanded in May 1919 but the station remained open until 1920. In the early 1920's the hanger was transported in its entirety to the seafront at Shanklin where it was used as a theatre, but in recent years has suffered the indignity of having a garish amusement arcade built in front of it.

In response to the increasing intensity of U-Boat operations in 1917 and 1918 it was decided to reinforce air cover resulting in opening of a landing ground variously known as New Bembridge or Forelands and occupying 51 acres of land immediately to the south of Lane End Road. Bessoneaux hangers were provided for the 12 de Havilland 6's based there from June 1918. The D.H.6 was both underpowered and inherently unstable and ditchings were not uncommon. It had a number of nicknames, two of the better known being "Clutching Hands" or "Sky Hook" but as usual the Australians were the most descriptive who christened it "Dung Hunter". With the formation of the Royal Air Force the unit became 511 and 512 Flights of 253 Squadron. The Station closed in 1919 and was sold in the following year, the R.A.F. apparently leaving it in a bad state. In 1918 another landing ground was opened on requisitioned land at Brading Haven, to the west of Home Farm and to the south of the St. Helens to Bembridge railway, but closed in 1919. Aircraft of 512 and 513 *(later A & B Flights)* from Forelands operated there from time to time.

Post World War I a number of Island gentry approached the owner of Bembridge Farm, a Mr E.U. Taylor with a view of providing land for a private airfield, Mr Taylor himself being interested in aviation agreed on a site to the north of the Bembridge - Sandown road; the landing ground was laid out in 1920 and was licenced in 1921. The project was a success and by the early 1930's there were three grass strips namely, NNE/SSW, E/W and N/S, the latter being 2,340 feet *(715m)* and by 1933 Bembridge had become an A.A. approved airfield. A hanger and terminal building were erected in 1934 and from the 1st May Spartan Airlines used Bembridge as an "On Request" on its Cowes - London route, but in 1935 this

was upgraded to a scheduled stop. Also in 1934 and 1935 Portsmouth, Southsea and Isle of Wight Aviation Ltd operated a direct Heston - Bembridge service and additionally the same company used it as an extension (on request) on its Portsmouth - Ryde Ferry. PSIOWA advertised it as Bembridge *(for Whitecliff Bay)*.

From May 1936 Channel Air Ferries used Bembridge as the Island stop on its Shoreham - Bembridge and later a Bournemouth service which provided connections to Bristol, Weston-Super-Mare and Cardiff.

At the outbreak of World War II the airfield was closed and on the 17th May 1940 a troop of the 10th Holding Company occupied the hanger by the simple expedient of breaking the padlocks. Three mechanical diggers were brought in and proceeded to plough trenches across the airfield, this task taking some ten weeks and in the process managing to break up the pre-war drainage system. The Air Ministry paid the owners £150 P.A. for the hanger and £200 P.A. for the land but they were somewhat recalcitrant in writing a cheque as the first payment was not received until 1943! The airfield was de-requisitioned in 1946 and compensation of £4,700 was paid in 1947. Since 1967 Bembridge has been the home of Britten-Norman *(now Pilatus Britten-Norman)*, the designers and builders of the famous Islander, Trilander and Defender series of aircraft. It is now the only airfield on the Island to offer a hard runway *(12/30, 913yds)* and full night flying facilities.

Cowes (Somerton) 5045N 0118W

The old established shipbuilders J. Samuel White Ltd had a long history to the extent they may well have built ships to combat the Spanish Armada but they made their name in later years by building fast cutters which could not be outrun and therefore were very popular with smugglers! To combat this the Treasury sanctioned the Customs to purchase the fastest possible cutters, and as such, had no choice but to order them from Whites! They built up a reputation for building destroyers, not only for the Royal Navy, but also for foreign Navies, and consequently they knew their way around the corridors of Admiralty power. Aviation in 1912 was very much in its infancy but the directors were far sighted and as they could see the day when aircraft would pose a threat to warships a decision was taken to establish an aviation division. The aircraft designer Howard T. Wright was appointed General Manager and Chief Designer and took up his new duties in November 1912, the board deciding that any aircraft that was built would not be known as Samuel White Aircraft but as a Wight Aircraft. This was a source of possible confusion as there was White, Wright and Wight.

*Operations Room
- Cowes 1936*

Credit:
Millichap/Croydon Airport Society

To clarify matters:-
White:- *J. Samuel White Ltd*
Wright:- *Howard T. - Designer*
Wight:- *Obviously from Isle of Wight - the base*

Due to the company's close relationship with the Admiralty they tended to concentrate on seaplanes such as their first aircraft, Wight Navyplane No 1 which crashed on its first flight. A modified design known as Navyplane No 2 was a success and was accepted by the Admiralty at Calshot until being written off in 1916. A considerable number of floatplanes were built up to 1916 and one of these, the Type 840 was an outstanding success. To capitalise on this the decision was taken to build a landplane version and although the company already possessed a flying field at Three Gates Cottages it was too small for large aircraft. They were successful in obtaining 60 acres at Somerton and a little later they acquired a further 20 acres on the other side of the

Cowes - Newport road on which a factory and workshops were built. The landplane version of the 840 flew successfully but being an adaption of an existing design it was becoming outdated and the Admiralty only ordered one which crashed on R.N.A.S. service in October 1916, the Admiralty not paying for it until some weeks after it was written off! A new landplane bomber was designed and known only as Type 9841, this being a single engine three bay biplane with a wingspan of 76 feet and fitted with racks to carry eight bombs. On its second flight on the 7th September 1916 it crashed at Gurnard killing the pilot Ralph Lashmar and his brother. This resulted in the Admiralty sending a demand for the cost of the bomb racks destroyed in the crash! From then on J. Samuel Whites tended to concentrate on seaplanes but one aeroplane of interest was the Quadruplane which was designed as a fighter to combat the Fokker Triplane, the theory being the greater number of wings, the better! Several variations were built but none went into production.

With the war ended the aircraft division closed down on the 28th July 1919 and during the 1920s the factory premises were rented out to a number of companies including the Vectis Bus Company who built their own bus bodies. Another organisation was the Scooter Motor company but little is known about them. In 1922/3 F. Warren Merriam based his gliding school at Somerton but this was not a success and the activity ceased after a short while. In 1925 S.E. Saunders Ltd *(Saro from 3rd July 1929)* took out a lease on Somerton for an initial five year period but was later extended and in the following year F. Warren Merriam opened his Aviation Employment Bureau which is believed to be the first in the country, if not the world. In the late 1920s Sir Alan Cobham visited in connection with his National Air Days as did another famous pioneering pilot C.D. Barnard with his Fokker VIIa "The Spider" G-EBTS. In 1929 Saro received an order to build sixty five Blackburn Bluebird IV side by side seating single engine all metal light touring biplanes, the reason for this sub-contracting being that Blackburn Aircraft of Brough, Yorkshire was fully committed to Military orders. At its peak production reached four per month but in fact only fifty five were built at Somerton and some of those were completed at Brough.

On the 30th July 1930 the pioneer airman Captain C.D. Barnard's Aerial Circus gave displays and joy rides. His aircraft were represented by his famous Fokker VIIa G-EBTS "The Spider" resplendent in its blue and silver livery. The previous April this aircraft made a record breaking flight from England to the Cape in 10 days, arriving on the 19th. On that occasion "The Spider" was flown by the Duchess of Bedford (Mary) with C.D. Barnard as co-pilot. Another of his aircraft that was present was the Cierva Autogiro C.19 Mark II G-AAYP.

Cowes 1936   Credit: Millichap/Croydon Airport Society

Also in 1929 Saro designed and built at Somerton a fighter to Air Ministry specification F20/27 which called for a fast interceptor but after testing at A and A.E.E. Martlesham Heath it was rejected in favour of the Hawker Fury. On the 12th August 1931 a successful Air Display was held and included a fly past by fifteen aircraft and Pauline Gower, the well known aviatrix gave rides in a Spartan Arrow.

In 1931 Spartan Aircraft moved to Somerton from Southampton, this company eventually being absorbed by Saro. Among the aircraft built by Spartan Saro were the Arrow and Three Seater, the Saro/Percival Mailplane, the three different marks of the Cruiser, the Spartan Clipper and the Saro/Segrave Meteor. On the 12th April 1933 Spartan Airlines (a subsidiary of Spartan Aircraft Ltd) commenced a Cowes - London (Heston) service using Spartan Cruiser I

G-ABTY but was later joined by Cruisers Mk II and III. The following year the London terminal became Croydon, in 1935 they moved back to Heston and in 1936 to Gatwick! To facilitate safe operations the Somerton windmill was demolished but this was not achieved without local resistance.

During World War II Somerton was the only Isle of Wight airfield that remained open as it was used for communications and for the flight testing of Saro built Walrus's. When not in use and to prevent hostile glider landings poles were inserted into the ground and sheep were allowed to graze. When an aircraft was expected two chaps on a motorcycle would pull up the poles and disperse the sheep with the aid of an old bulb type motor horn! Post war Somerton was used by various operators but closed in 1952.

Midland 7 Scottish Air Ferries Dragon at Cowes

Credit: John King

Monospar of Provincial Airways at Portsmouth, note 4-bladed propellers

Credit: 'The News', Portsmouth

Portsmouth Airport

Credit: Hewes, Portsmouth

In 1959 Decca Radar (now Siemens Plessey) moved in and is now a significant employer on the Island. Saro was taken over by the British Hovercraft Corporation, itself a subsidiary of Westland Aerospace, and they bought the land from J. Samuel White Ltd in 1966. The factory on the other side of the road still exists and is used by light industry. During its history the airfield has been called by various names including:- Cowes, Cowes (Somerton), Somerton, Northwood, West Wight and by the R.A.F as simply Wight Airfield.

Portsmouth
5050N 0103E
2.5 miles NE of the City centre
In June 1919 the City entered into an agreement with a Mr E.J. Hucks (the agent for Avro Ltd) to operate joy riding facilities from Southsea Common, part of the agreement being that 33% of the profits would be for the benefit of the War Memorial fund, but the outcome was not satisfactory and the City terminated the agreement on the 26th July. Completely unabashed Mr Hucks then applied for permission to operate a seaplane from South Parade Pier and surprisingly this was granted with operations commencing on the 2nd August, this also was not a success and the City terminated the agreement only twenty days later. The next operator on the scene was Surrey Flying Services who applied for permission to operate from Southsea Common, not unnaturally this was refused but nevertheless the Corporation indicated that they would view with favour an

application to operate from Great Salterns to the north of the City and on the west shore of Langstone Harbour. this was granted and became effective for the period 1st May to the 30th September. Surrey Flying Services operated Avro 504's and 536's and whilst the financial outcome is not known it must have been satisfactory as they stayed the full period of the agreement.

In response to the Air Ministry letter of 1928 addressed to all cities and towns with a population of 20,000 or more pointing out the advantages of having a municipal airport, Portsmouth Corporation set up a committee and appointed Mr Nigel Norman (later Sir) of Norman Muntz and Partners to advise them. A site was chosen to the north of the City and under the Portsmouth Corporation Act of 1930 land totalling 275 acres, including Highgrove Farm, was compulsorily purchased, the contract being awarded to the well known airport constructors Messrs Hunters of Chester and Frank Bevis Ltd of Portsmouth. To the north of the site there were old Napoleonic fortifications, including very substantial ramparts, and the removal of them was a major undertaking, the construction of the airport taking in the excess of two years. The actual work qualified for the Government unemployment Relief Scheme and the buildings consisted of a terminal block which included a 100 seater restaurant, a customs office and administration offices. A clubhouse was created by converting and extending a farmhouse, a hanger built to accommodate up to eight light aircraft and a larger hanger measuring 130ft x 120ft for commercial use, this being tenanted by PSIOWA.

Jersey Airways DH86 'St Catherine's Bay' at Portsmouth   Credit: The News, Portsmouth

On the 2nd July 1932 the airport was officially opened by Sir Phillip Sassoon, Under Secretary for State for Air deputising for the Marquess of Londonderry who had been called away abroad on Government business. The Lord Mayor and the Lady Mayoress Mr and Mrs F.G. Foster were flown around the City in an Armstrong Whitworth Argosy. A crowd of over 50,000 witnessed the event and over 100 aircraft participated. Displays were given by Hawker Furies of 1 and 43 Squadrons from Tangmere led by the Squadron Leader Hanmer M.C. An aerobatic display was given by Tiger Moths of the Central Flying School and there was a fly past of various aircraft. Among the aircraft present were Vickers Virginias, the C.D. Barnard's famous Fokker VII "The Spider", the Westland Pterodactyl and numerous light aircraft. There were the air races namely, the Grosvenor Cup, the S.B.A.C. Challenge Trophy and the Portsmouth Challenge Cup. The first being won by C.S Napier in a Westland Widgeon G-AADE, the S.B.A.C. Trophy by W.E. Johnson in a D.H.60 Moth G-AAJJ and the Portsmouth Challenge by C. Birkett in a Monocoupe G-ABBR of Air Taxis Ltd. In the evening the Graf Zeppelin flew over and rumours developed that it wasn't so much a mission of goodwill but its primary purpose was to obtain photographs of the R.N. Dockyard.

Before the airport was officially opened PSIOWA commenced schedules operations with the Ryde Ferry using the Wessex G-ABVB. On the 19th August Sir Alan Cobham arrived with his Air Circus and praised the facilities at the new airport, and on the 21st of the same month PSIOWA

started a "Round the Island" air tour departing Portsmouth every evening at 17.00. On the 5th September the same company started a Shoreham - Portsmouth - Ryde service.

In March 1933 Airspeed transferred from York, Portsmouth Corporation building them a new factory. The first aircraft assembled at Portsmouth (it was partially built at York) was the prototype Courier G-ABXN which was later used by Sir Alan Cobham for flight refuelling and in 1939 by PSIOWA. By that year Airspeed, after the Royal Naval Dockyard and the Council, had become the largest employer in Portsmouth and there is little doubt that the City had done a good job in wooing them. On the 16th June 1933 a new clubhouse was opened for the PSIOWA founded Portsmouth Aero Club, the ceremony being conducted by the Lord Mayor Councillor W.A. Billing, the charges being 50/- (£2.50) per hour dual and 30/- (£1.50) solo. The Portsmouth Aero Club also incorporated the Royal Navy Flying Club which did not possess any aircraft! During 1933 Portsmouth installed passenger boarding gates which were believed to be the first in the country, number one being Ryde Ferry, Number two Shanklin Ferry, Number three Shoreham Ferry, Number four Pleasure Flights and Number five was a spare.

On the 24th August a new airline, International Airlines, commenced a new service from Croydon to Portsmouth - Southampton and Plymouth but the airline ceased operations after twenty days. On the 6th September the Portsmouth Aero Club organised an Isle of Wight Handicap Race, it being won by Sir Charles Rose flying a D.H. 60G Moth

G-AAKN. On the 18th December Jersey Airways started daily Portsmouth - Jersey services using D.H. Dragon G-ACMJ plus another unidentified Dragon but as they had to land on the beach in Jersey the schedule was at the mercy of the tide.

In 1934 Airspeed experienced severe financial problems and were taken over by the well known Tyneside shipbuilders Swan Hunter Wigham Richardson Ltd, the company being reconstituted as Airspeed *(1934)* Ltd. In the same year Antony Fokker, the famous Dutch aircraft designer, obtained the European manufacturing rights for the Douglas DC2 Transport and approached Airspeed with a proposition to build this aircraft at Portsmouth. His terms were considered outrageous as he wanted £20,000 up front, another £20,000 when turnover reached £100,000, and one percent commission on sales plus 50,000 shares. Despite this Fokker was taken on as consultant but to make matters worse Airspeed's solicitors failed to insert a clause restricting payments only to Fokker designs and introductions, this failure meaning that Fokker benefited from profits on the Oxford. Airspeed only managed to get rid of him by invoking the Official Secrets Act and as an alien and one time enemy he was barred from the boardroom.

In 1934 PSIOWA expanded once again by introducing a Shoreham - Portsmouth - Bournemouth service. With increasing activity plus the new airway between Portsmouth and the Island radio was becoming essential and a mobile radio station was installed, frequency 862 metres, callsign "Portsmouth."

PSIOWA organised two "Round the Island" races, the major of the two being twice round the Island and the other a single circuit to compete for the Portsmouth Trophy. Two trophies were offered for the major race, namely the Duckham, designed for commercial pilots (holders of "B" licences) and the Peters Trophy for "A" licence pilots. The Duckhams Trophy was won by Mr R.P. Pope the C.F.I. of Air Training Ltd at Hamble flying Comper Swift G-ACML. The Peters Trophy was awarded to Mr F.S. Cotton in Avro Avian IV M G-ABME and the Portsmouth Trophy was won by PSIOWA director F.L. Luxmoore in a D.H. 60G Moth G-AAKN.

During 1934 Provincial Airlines used Portsmouth as an intermediary stop on its Croydon - Plymouth route. On the 21st September Sir Alan Cobham attempted a non stop Portsmouth - Karachi flight in Airspeed Courier G-ABXN utilising his pioneering flight refuelling technique, the intention being to refuel over Malta and Alexandria but a broken throttle linkage forced him to land at the former and abandon the attempt.

On the 22nd July 1935 PSIOWA inaugurated the first international service from Portsmouth using a new Airspeed Envoy G-ADCA on its Paris service but this apparently was not a success and the operation ceased after two months. The mobile radio station installed in 1934 was replaced by a more powerful permanent installation in July 1935.

Portsmouth was also the venue of what had to be one of the first hijackings. On the 20th August 1936 two employees of Airspeed named A. Garratt and J.A. Smith who had never flown before, stole an Airspeed Courier G-ACVE with the idea of selling it in Spain and drawing a fat cheque. Their one and only navigation aid was a school atlas and the plan was to fly to the French coast and then turn right! The aircraft crashed on take off, Garratt subsequently dying of his injuries. The crime of Air Piracy had not then been enacted and Smith was charged with larceny, breaking and entering and was sentenced to three months. The authorities had suspicions that Airspeed "Had been looking the other way" resulting in the local Constabulary dispatching a veritable "posse" to oversee activities. One engineer wished to taxi an aircraft to the flight shed but could only do so if accompanied by two policemen, one inside and the other sitting on the tail. The engineer neglected to inform the latter that it was his normal practice to taxi at 40mph!

In 1936 Portsmouth hosted the Schlesinger England to Johannesburg Race and one competitor was the locally built Airspeed Envoy G-AENA "Gabrielle" which was entered by Max Findlay and Ken Waller. The other members of the crew were A.H. Morgan (radio operator) and C.D. Peachey (engineer). Tragically, the Envoy crashed on take off at Abercorn killing Findlay and Morgan, the other two occupants being practically uninjured.

During the year much consideration was given to a flying boat base in adjacent Langstone Harbour but this was shelved only to be raised again in 1937 at an estimated cost of £1,200,000; the Government subsidy was less than originally anticipated and was never implemented. According to the Portsmouth Evening News of 14th February 1937, an Imperial Airways Empire Flying Boat visited Langstone Harbour and in the same month a Swissair D.C.2 paid a call but for what purpose is not known. In 1938 Portsmouth Aero Club was awarded a contract under the Civil Air Guard scheme which was designed to train would-be pilots for the R.A.F. at subsidised rates and by 1939 Portsmouth Aero Club had flown more CAG hours than any other club in the country. Out of a total of 8,586 Oxfords produced, 4,411 were built at Portsmouth. During the war Airspeed carried on with production of Oxford and Horsa gliders and PSIOWA (from 1943 Portsmouth Aviation Ltd) repaired over 5,000 aircraft.

Post war a number of operators used Portsmouth, the principal one being Channel Airways who initially flew Dakotas. In June 1949 an R.A.F. Anson failed to stop on the wet grass and ended up on the main Portsmouth - London railway shorting out the current, all occupants escaping before the Anson caught fire. On May 6th 1962 a Channel Airways Dakota G-AGZB inbound to Portsmouth collided with St Boniface Down on the Isle of Wight but remarkably six persons survived out of seventeen. The airport was always susceptible to waterlogging and on the 15th August 1967 a Channel Airways HS748 G-ATEK skidded and ended up on the river bank at the north end of the airport. Some ninety minutes later another Channel Airways HS748 G-ATEH also failed to stop and came to rest across the main Eastern Road. These accidents a caused a review to be made in regard to the future of the airport but constrained by physical barriers to the south, the west and the north, the only option was to build a hard runway out into Langstone Harbour. The cost of dredging and piling was prohibitive and the airport closed on the 31st December 1973, the last aircraft to land being Prestwick Twin Pioneer G-AYSS of J.F. Airlines.

Ryde

5042N 0108W

Although Wight Aviation Ltd had a successful two seasons offering joyriding, air taxis and flying instruction at Shanklin (Apse) their intention was to develop an air ferry to the Island and it was obvious that Apse would not be suitable for passenger aircraft that were coming on the market. An alternative had therefore to be found, the criteria being near the centres of population such as Ryde, Sandown and Shanklin and with unobstructed approaches. A site was found at Barnsley Farm and Wight Aviation Ltd opened negotiations with the farmer, a Mr M.V. Faithful, agreement was reached and 82 acres were sold to the company for a freehold price of £12,000. The site was immediately to the east of the main Ryde to Sandown road and was one and a half miles from the centre of the former. Wight Aviation took possession in March 1932 and preparations to convert the site into an airfield was the responsibility of Hunters of Chester, who at that time were the premier airport contractors (they were also preparing Portsmouth at the same time). In order to reflect the company's aspirations Wight Aviation Ltd changed its name in April 1932 to "Portsmouth, Southsea and Isle Wight Aviation Ltd" (PSIOWA). The first scheduled flight to the Island by anyone took place on the 27th June with PSIOWA's new Wessex G-ABVB which flew in from Portsmouth to inaugurate the initial four times daily service. From that date services gradually built up with Shoreham being added in September and from summer 1933 Spartan Airlines used Ryde as a stop on its Cowes - Heston route. In 1934 new airport buildings were commissioned, the design of

which were overseen by F.L. Luxmoore of PSIOWA and by the end of July they were officially opened. They consisted of a booking hall and check in, restaurant, waiting room, a staff room, a staff office and a control tower. The construction was carried out by the well known structural engineers and aircraft builders, Boulton & Paul of Norwich.

The timing of the completion of this complex coincided with the start of a twice daily Railway Air Service route initially from Birmingham, Bristol, Southampton, Ryde and then on to Shoreham. Also by this time PSIOWA had started a direct Heston - Ryde service using D.H.84 Dragon II G-ACRF. On Saturday 8th July 1934 an Armstrong Whitworth Argosy G-AACJ "City of Manchester" of Imperial Airways landed at Ryde with a full load of passengers on a day charter from Croydon, this being the largest aircraft to land there to date. Ryde was increasingly used by various airlines and by May 1936 and agreement was reached between PSIOWA and Railway Air Services (with Channel Air Ferries joining later) that Ryde be designated as the principal Island airport. There were a number of reasons for this, not the least it being virtually fog free with good approaches. Combined with this was that it was near a large town, it was just off the main road to the holiday resorts of Sandown and Shanklin and it had superior passenger handling facilities. In 1937 the owners (PSIOWA) transferred the ownership to a wholly owned subsidiary, described as an airport management company, named "Vectis Airports Ltd". In July of that year passenger demand was such that on occasions passengers had to queue for the Portsmouth Ferry and on flights to other destinations some would-be passengers were turned away.

There is no doubt that Ryde Airport was an outstanding success and in terms of aircraft and passenger movements. It certainly challenged Portsmouth as the leading airport in the South, the figures for 1938 and 1939 were:-

Aircraft movements	Passengers
	1938
6,953	30,910
	1939
7,848	37,621

Due to the outbreak of War on the 3rd September, the figures for 1939 cover only eleven months.

On the 8th and 9th August 1939 the R.A.F. arrived in the form of two Bristol Bombays which landed to uplift troops for an exercise on Salisbury Plain. The airport closed on 3rd September 1939 but it may have re-opened briefly after the War. The site is now occupied by a Leisure Centre and a supermarket that trades under the name of Tesco, the control tower surviving until finally demolished in recent years.

Island Flying Club's Prototype General Aircraft Cygnet G-AEMA at Sandown, 1936   Credit: Henry Nobbs

Sandown (Lea)

In 1934 Mr E. Byrne having failed in his efforts to buy Languard Manor bought 161 acres of Lea Farm, Sandown and during the winter of 34/35 work commenced on removing 2,000 yards of hedging, levelling and the demolition of some 300 year old farm buildings. In February 1935, and before the airport was opened, Byrne formed Sandown and Shanklin Flying Services thus absorbing the original Coombs Shanklin Flying Services and took over two of his three original aircraft namely:- Spartan Three Seater G-ABAZ "Island Queen" and Spartan Arrow G-AAWY, both of which were prototypes. The airport opened at Easter 1935 with a grass runway of 1,170 yards in the direction of S.W./N.E. On Empire Air Day in June the new airport was officially inspected by Mr A.J. Mew, President of the Isle of Wight Chamber of Commerce, Mr A.J. Harman and Mr N. Douglas Best, respectively Chairman and Joint Clerk to the Sandown/Shanklin District Council and Mr W.A. Dobson, Entertainments Manager. They were conducted around the airport by Mr E.H. Byrne, Managing Director of Shanklin and Sandown Flying Services and Mr W.A. Andrews C.F.I., also present were Mr C. Grasemann and Mr J.E.Bell, both representing the Southern Railway and Mr W.A. Budd of Southern Vectis. A Spartan Cruiser was flown over from Cowes to enable the party to inspect the interior, but this was not as has been suggested, an inaugural flight as Spartan did not commence services from Sandown until the 1st July.

Spartan Air Lines indicated their willingness to use the new airport and a hanger was built for them which was completed in May. Spartan opened a direct London (Heston) - Sandown service between 1st July and the 15th September with a frequency of up to four flights per day with an extra flight on Saturdays. The total time between Victoria Coach Station and Sandown was 1 hour 40 minutes with an actual flight time of 45 minutes. over the August Bank Holiday Spartan carried some 210 passengers which was good going for aircraft with a passenger capacity of only eight. On the 13th August Sir Alan Cobham's Air Circus gave a display which apparently was well attended. In November 1935 Byrne formed the Isle of Wight Flying Club which should not be confused with the original Wight Aviation Island Flying Club at Apse which due to that company's *(now PSIOWA)* concentration on scheduled services had been allowed to wither on the vine. The new Isle of Wight Flying Club was incorporated with a paid up capital of £100 and had 50 founder members. The clubhouse was officially opened on the 25th July 1936 by the Island M.P. Captain Peter McDonald and representatives of the flying clubs of Portsmouth, Redhill and Southend attended. A frequent visitor was the famous actress and comedienne, Jeanne de Casales who, when performing at Shanklin Theatre, piloted a General Aircraft Monospar.

From the 7th July 1937 PSIOWA operated a twice daily Portsmouth - Sandown service and this continued until the outbreak of war. In September 1938 the Isle of Wight Flying Club was successful in becoming a member of the Government subsidised Civil Air Guard scheme and within one month had 130 volunteers. The fees for "standard" aircraft were 5/- *(25p)* per hour mid-week and 10/- at weekends, the corresponding fees for "light" aircraft were 2/6d *(12½p)* and 5/- *(25p)* and in the seven months preceding the outbreak of war a total of 56 members obtained their licences. Aircraft operated by the club included de Havilland 60 Moths G-EBRY, G-AAAL, G-AABJ, G-ABBX, G-ABLN and G-ABPD plus Avro Avians G-AAWH and G-ABIW. A DH Fox Moth G-ACEA was used for joy riding. An unusual aircraft that was also operated was the prototype General Aircraft Cygnet prototype G-AEMA , this type being the only British production aircraft at that time equipped with a tricycle undercarriage. During the War Cygnets were used by the R.A.F. to convert pilots onto the Douglas Boston bombers.

Sandown was closed during the war and as an anti invasion measure trenches were dug across the runways. The airfield re-opened in 1948 and was named the Isle of Wight Airport and apart from a period between 1974 when it closed and late 1976 when it re-opened Sandown expanded under new ownership, the airport has gone from strength to strength and today has a control tower and a number of hangers.

Shoreham (Brighton, Hove and Worthing)

Shoreham has a justified claim to be Britain's oldest licenced civil airport as its origins go back to 1909 when a local solicitor G.A. Wingfield took out a six months lease from the farmer of New Salts Farm, the land in question being bounded by the river to the east and the railway to the south. Wingfield had a friend, H.H. Piffard, who was a local artist and maker of model aeroplanes and together they formed Aviation Finance Ltd. Piffard built a full size aeroplane but this, along with its shed, was wrecked in a gale but undeterred he built a second aeroplane and after several abortive hops were made, the first proper flight was not until 10th July 1910. The following month young Stanley Vincent and his parents spent some time watching Piffard making preparations. His father, who was a Doctor of Music, used his tuning fork to help Piffard tune his 40 hp ENV engine. It has been suggested that this was the origin of the expression "Tuning up!" Master Stanley Vincent became a pupil of nearby Lancing College, after which he joined the R.A.F .and retired as Air Marshal Vincent CB, DFC, AFC.

On 11th March 1911 the pioneer airman Oscar Morison arrived at Shoreham from Brighton and made Shoreham his future base. Morison appeared to have plenty of funds as he had already written off several aeroplanes, and in the following month he had yet another accident when he crashed at Eastbourne. In June he survived a spectacular cartwheel at Brooklands, the final incident occurring in August when his Bleriot Monoplane ditched off Ventnor, Isle of Wight. The Bleriot was salvaged, overhauled and sold to W. Rhodes-Moorhouse who was the first member of the R.F.C. to be awarded posthumously the V.C. After the Ventnor mishap. Morison was rapidly running out of aircraft or funds and after he married in November 1912 he never flew again.

Wingfield began developing Shoreham by filling in some of the ditches making a landing run of some 2,000ft in a North-South direction, its boundaries were roughly those of the future municipal airport of 1935. On June 20th 1911 the Mayors of Brighton, Hove and Worthing officially opened Shoreham, G.A. Wingfield had in the meantime attracted several companies to the aerodrome including the British and Colonial Aeroplane Company Ltd (later Bristols) and one individual who would become well known for designing and testing namely Eric Gordon England. On July 4th 1911 a Horatio Barber flew what is the World's first recorded air cargo flight when he carried Osram lamps from Shoreham to Hove, landing in Marine Park, Wish Road, the consignment being on behalf of the General Electric Light Company Ltd who had organised an Electric Congress. He designed and built the aeroplane himself which was a tail first Canard Two Seater powered by a 50hp Gnome engine and named Valkyrie B. He received a fee of £100 for the flight and today this is commemorated by roads "Shoreham East" and "Shoreham West" at Heathrow Cargo Terminal.

On July 24th 1911 Claude Graham-White flew his Farman Pusher "Wake up England" in a private race between himself and a local hotelier in a motor cruiser from Black Rock to Portslade. The hotelier, Harry Preston, won by 10 yards!

In November 1911 the Chanter School of Flying moved to Shoreham from Hendon, bringing with them their two Bleriots but their term was short lived as in February 1912 a fire destroyed the sheds housing their aeroplanes. In October 1912 a Mr H. Gonne was appointed Aerodrome Manager and was largely instrumental in enticing Brooklands based AVRO's to Shoreham where not only could they carry out their well established Flying School but could test seaplanes in the nearby River Adur. One of their instructors was John Alcock who became famous for the first trans Atlantic crossing in 1919 flying a Vickers Vimy with Arthur Whitten-Brown. Shoreham had by the end of 1912 a clubhouse/pavilion, a restaurant, tennis courts and a croquet lawn.

Terminal Buildings Shoreham 1938 Credit: Shoreham Airport Collection

Terminal Buildings Shoreham 1938 Credit: Shoreham Airport Collection

About this time the Pashley brothers Cecil and Eric arrived at Shoreham and founded the Sussex County Aero Club, the latter losing his life in 1917 while serving with the R.F.C. Cecil, although he carried on instructing at other venues returned to Shoreham in 1921 and by then had amassed 6,000 hours of instructional time. He stayed at Shoreham until well after World War II and by the time the authorities revoked his licence in December 1965 (*he was 74*) he had spent nearly sixty years in aviation, most of the time instructing, he appealed against the revocation and the authorities relented on condition that he always flew with another licenced pilot. Returning to the early years, a James Radley began working on a new project and in the early stages he was joined by Eric Gordon England who apart from being a pioneer aviator was later to achieve recognition as a designer. They produced the Radley-England Waterplane powered by three Gnome rotary 50hp engines in three banks, which driving a single crankshaft, which in turn drove a nine foot ten inch propeller. Each of the twin floats had three seats and it was flown from the front seat of the right hand float. Gordon England made a successful flight from off Brighton beach on the 1st May 1933 but unfortunately upon alighting the starboard float struck a marker buoy and the machine sank. Undeterred it was salvaged and rebuilt with stronger floats and powered this time by a single 150hp Sunbeam V8, the engineer who assisted in fitting this engine being John Alcock. Thus modified it was named Waterplane II but was not a success as the design of the floats was such that it had difficulty in unsticking. Radley, quite wrongly, blamed the Sunbeam engine which caused much bitterness and John Alcock departed the scene. In the meantime Avro pilot Fred Raynham tested the Avro 503 floatplane from the River Adur but on a later flight he suffered engine failure just after take off and at the time he was heading for the railway bridge but managed to fly between one of the arches. When the mechanics later measured the arch they found the clearance at the wingtips was nine inches and only six inches above! The Avro flying school left Shoreham in September 1913 as there had been complaints about their aircraft, their Chief Pilot having departed earlier. Undeterred by the failure of the Waterplane, James Radley built the unusual Annular Monoplane designed by G.T. Richards and Cedric Lee, Gordon England being retained as test pilot at the rate of ten pounds an hour. He carried out a few exploratory hops on 23rd November 1913, suddenly found himself airborne and so carried on for forty five minutes, but on the approach the engine failed and he lost control, the aircraft performing a complete roll before crashing alongside the railway line, Gordon England sustaining a damaged knee and was on crutches for several weeks. The findings were that the centre of gravity was too far aft but the designers claimed that annular planes were more stable due to the vortex effect of the eleven foot diameter hole. According to Charles Gates

when the aerodrome was waterlogged a definite spume of water could be seen going up through the hole when taxied at speed!

On the 4th August 1914 war with Germany was declared but private flying continued until December when Major Gerrard of the Royal Marines requisitioned the airfield and all aircraft. Wingfield had all his assets seized and commenced proceedings against the Government for compensation but the High Court found against him and he was forced to appeal to the Lords, they found in his favour and was awarded £25,000 which enabled him to clear his debts. In January 1915 the R.F.C. arrived at Shoreham as No 3 Reserve Squadron, their function being basic flying training. During that year ninety seven pupils passed out including Sholto Douglas who was to become an Air Chief Marshal and Harold Balfour who became Under Secretary of State for Air (later Lord Balfour of Inchrye). Such were the losses on the Western Front that in 1917 the flying training syllabus was reduced to three hours dual followed by three hours solo!

In April 1918 No 1 and No 2 Squadrons of the Canadian Air Force moved in, the former flying S.E.5A's and the latter with D.H.9A's. No 1 Squadron was later equipped with Sopwith Dolphins but both Squadrons were disbanded by the end of February 1921. Shoreham had on charge some sixty five captured enemy aircraft and these were gifted to Canada by the British Government. The aerodrome then reverted to agricultural use.

In 1925 Cecil Pashley met Fred Miles who would become famous as one of the leading light aircraft designers in the country and together they formed the Gnat Aero Company. They managed to talk the farmer into renting a field which they had to share with his cows; their Avro 504K had been overhauled in the Star laundry and they entered the joy riding business but Fred Miles had yet to learn to fly. Pashley acted as his instructor and Miles gained his "A" licence in June 1926. In the meantime they found a larger field north of the railway and plans were made to build hangers and a clubhouse but with only one aircraft they were vulnerable; to rectify this they acquired an Avro Baby and made up another 504K from spares. These activities came to the notice of the authorities as Pashley was the only one to have a "B" licence, there were no licenced ground engineers and Certificates of Airworthiness tended to be overlooked! They received a rocket from the Air Ministry but carried on and to improve the coffers decided to hold an air display. An hour before the display was due to start a Bristol fighter landed and out stepped Sir Sefton Brancker, the Director of Civil Aviation. Miles welcomed him and offered him a drink but Sir Sefton announced "So this is the headquarters of the Independent Air Force, no licences, no certificates of airworthiness, no inspections". Sir Sefton, of course, had the power to close them down immediately but was satisfied with Miles undertaking to put their house in order. The business was then split with Southern Aircraft Ltd being responsible for maintenance and the Southern Aero Club handling the training and joy riding. In 1929 Miles borrowed £7,000 from the bank, guaranteed by his father, to buy the freehold of the original field as a speculation. On the 5th September 1932 PSIOWA commenced a route from Shoreham to Portsmouth and Ryde. Also in this year Sir Alan Cobham arrived with his Handley Page W.10 G-EBMR for national aviation displays. He was asked by the three local authorities to recommend a site for a possible Municipal Airport and he suggested the original 1911 airfield. The Joint Airport Committee bought the 147 acre site from Miles for £10,000 thus making him a profit of £3,000! A further £31,000 was allocated for a terminal building and hangers. Work commenced in November 1934, the terminal building being built in the "Art Deco" style with plans for four hangers, but only one was built. By this time Miles had left Shoreham to build up his company at Woodley but flew in with his Merlin displaying U.8 markings but which later became G-ADFE. Olley Air Services were appointed managers of the airport with Captain the Earl Amhurst M.C. as General Manager. The Southern Aero Club was re-organised as the South Coast Flying Club under the control of Brooklands Aviation Ltd and a clubhouse was established on the first floor of the terminal building with Cecil Pashley as C.F.I., the old Southern Aircraft Ltd being wound up. The club's aircraft were painted in an attractive colour scheme with black fuselage with red upper decking, the wings silver with red registration letters. The airport was officially opened on the 13th June 1936 by the Mayors of Brighton, Hove and Worthing and an aerobatic display was given by 19 Squadron R.A.F. flying Gloster Gauntletts led by Flight Lt. H. Broadhurst (later Air Chief Marshal Sir Harry Broadhurst). Other events included a demonstration of a Belgium registered *(OO-ELA)* 1912 Caudron G3 by Ken Waller and a fly past consisting of a Percival Vega Gull, a Stinson, Hester Phoenix, a B.A. Swallow and Eagle, a Miles Falcon 6, and an aerobatic display by an Avro Cadet flown by S.A. (Bill) Thorn who was later to become Chief Test Pilot of Avro's but was killed flying the prototype Tudor II. Airlines now operating from and to Shoreham were PSIOWA, RAS, Cobham Air Routes and Jersey Airways with Channel Air Ferries opening a route to Ryde and Bournemouth in 1936, all of which reflected Shoreham's increasing importance. With an increasing threat of war, the Air Ministry contracted the Martin School of Navigation to train RAFVR pilots using Tiger Moths, Hawker Hinds and Harts. In 1938 this was extended to observer training utilising DH89a Rapides, a DH84 Dragon and Fairey Battles, but subsequently the Air Ministry became

dissatisfied with Martin's performance which resulted in the contract for observer training being cancelled and awarded to Airwork at Staverton. In March 1939 RAS was split between the railways resulting in Channel Air Ferries coming under the umbrella of the new railway airline, Great Western and Southern Airlines.

On the outbreak of war, all private flying ceased but Shoreham was used, instead of Croydon, by airlines of the then neutral countries of Denmark, Holland and Belgium. Today Shoreham is still thriving but this is a book about pre-war activities and anybody who wishes to research Shoreham in its entirety should obtain a copy of "Shoreham Airport Sussex" by T.M.A. Webb and Dennis L. Bird. This publication can be considered a definitive history.

Southampton (Eastleigh)

In 1910 occasional flights took place at the North Stoneham Farm watermeadows which are between the London - Southampton railway line and Wide Lane (A335). A local businessman, Eric Moon, who ran a marine engineering company named Moonbeams Ltd, had offices at Royal Pier Gates and workshops at the old Wool House *(now the Maritime Museum),* became interested in aviation and built several aeroplanes. It is believed his first successful flight was from Paultons Park, Ower, but he was certainly the first to fly a powered machine from Eastleigh. This was an aeroplane of his own design with a 24 foot wingspan and powered by a four cylinder 20hp Jap engine. It was named Moonbeam II. On the outbreak of war in 1914 he was commissioned in the R.N.A.S. and saw service in East Africa. He survived the war only to be killed in 1920 flying a Felixstowe flying boat.

In 1910/11 the field was used by Graham White and Maurice Tetard. The field then tended to lapse into disuse, but some time after the war broke out the R.F.C. established a depot at Leigh Road, and in 1917 it was decided to use the airfield as an aircraft acceptance park. The land was requisitioned, work commenced on the construction of four large hangers and five storage sheds, all being built alongside the railway line. Before work was completed the Air Ministry was approached by the U.S. Government to recommend a site for assembly of U.S. built de Havilland 4's with Eastleigh being offered and accepted. The U.S. Navy Northern Bombing Group moved in on the 20th July 1918, but the D.H.4's did not appear on time so a deal was done whereby the British supplied 54 D.H.9A's in exchange for Liberty engines. These aircraft were assembled and flight tested at Eastleigh and then sent to France to equip the 10th Bombing Unit. At the Armistice in November of that year, the U.S. Navy was responsible for collecting and dispatching supplies back to the United States with final withdrawal in April 1919.

Eastleigh was then handed back to the Air Ministry who closed the station in May 1920. In 1921 a shipping consortium leased the buildings as accommodation for European immigrants awaiting passage to the U.S.A. and named it the Atlantic Park Hostel.

During the 1920's Eastleigh became an unlicenced landing ground and in 1926 was used by Surrey Flying Services for joyriding who carried 3,600 passengers. In the late 1920's the Southern Railway who owned Southampton Docks decided on an expansion scheme along the mudflats of the Test. The scheme involved 1½ miles of quays and a graving dock designed to take the largest ships. The City Corporation were obviously very pleased with this development and to complement it, planning was commenced on the layout and design of a municipal airport. In 1929 the City Corporation bought 100 acres of land and started negotiations for the purchase of the buildings. Work started in early 1932 and immediately Vickers Supermarine indicated interest for flight testing purposes.

For such activity Air Ministry approval was required and the R.A.E. at Farnborough was given the responsibility of the inspection. This was satisfactory and sanction was given for use as a licenced private airport. Vickers Supermarine moved in during September and the airport was officially opened in November. From that date it was known as Southampton *(Eastleigh)* Airport with the Hampshire Aero Club moving in from Hamble.

The first scheduled service at Eastleigh was International Airlines which in August 1933 started a Croydon - Plymouth service with stops at Portsmouth or Southampton. This was, however, short-lived as they ceased operations after only twenty days. The next airline was Provincial Airways who from the 19th March 1934 operated a similar route to the above and continued to do so until they, in turn, ceased operations in September in the following year. On the 30th July 1934 Railway Air Services called at Southampton on their Birmingham - Bristol - Cowes route and would continue to do so until August 1938 when the route was taken over by Great Western and Southern Airlines, which as the name implies, was owned by the Great Western and Southern Railways. Another airline that used Southampton from 1934 was Jersey Airways and operated up to the early part of the War. During the winter of 1935/36 Spartan called at Southampton (weekdays only) on its seven day week service from the Isle of Wight to Heston.

With the installation of radio at Portsmouth in 1934, and in order to assist aircraft in bad weather, an arrangement was made between the two airports whereby the "Controller" at Eastleigh upon hearing an aircraft would immediately telephone Portsmouth who would endeavour to make contact and relay the aircraft's position. The Eastleigh "Controller" would then inform Portsmouth that judging by the sound of engines the aircraft was, say, north of the airport and Portsmouth would than pass this information to the pilot. It would appear that system worked reasonably well, but it must have come as a relief to all concerned when radio was installed at Eastleigh in 1936!

1936 was an eventful year with the Spitfire making its first flight and production commencing, although the majority of the Spitfires were built, not at Eastleigh, but the new Shadow factory at Castle Bromwich. In this year Cunliffe Owen started operations by building the Burnelli OA-1 Flying Wing which, in the event, did not sell. Another company was Foster, Wikner Aircraft Company Ltd who designed and built a single engine high wing monoplane and which was reasonably successful, production commencing in the following year. 1935/6 saw the upgrading of the airport with night flying facilities including three 11 million candle power floodlights and a beacon flashing "SN". Boundary and obstruction lights were installed as was a D/F radio station *(322kcs)* callsign GJD.

Another company which operated at Eastleigh from 1935 - 1939 was Portsmouth, Southsea and Isle of Wight Aviation Ltd. In 1935 they started a service to Ryde and Shanklin with four flights per day and in the following year they also operated a service to Cowes. In 1938 the Ryde service was upgraded to seven flights per day and this service, for the first time, operated through the winter of 38/39 at a reduced frequency. This company also used Eastleigh for their anti aircraft contract for A.A. gun practice. The Fleet Air Arm moved in to the north eastern sector and constructed a dummy carrier landing strip. The base was later *(1938)* commissioned as H.M.S. Raven, the airfield also being known as R.A.F. Southampton. 814 Squadron F.A.A. was formed in 1938 with twelve Swordfish and after working up embarked in H.M.S. Ark Royal. During 1938 811, 812 and 821 Swordfish Squadrons arrived but did not stay long as they embarked in August, Raven becoming an Observers School. In April a larger hanger was erected and a terminal was planned but did not materialise. The R.A.F. initially ordered two hundred Spitfires but there were production bottlenecks, this being partially overcome by Vickers taking over the Cunliffe Owen hanger. Their Burnelli Flying Wing first flew on the 12th January 1939 and an attempt was made to sell it to Gordon Olley for his Isle of Man service but this did not transpire and it was later scrapped. During the War Cunliffe Owen was kept busy making Spitfire components and assembling American aircraft arriving by sea. They were also heavily engaged in conversions to Lancasters for maritime duties and played a significant development role in the Uffa Fox designed Airborne Lifeboat. In September 1940 the Luftwaffe bombed their works killing some fifty people and later in the month Heinkel III's of KG55 completely destroyed the Supermarine works at Woolston. A balloon barrage was in place at Eastleigh but one of their first casualties appears to have been a OTU Hudson. The airfield was obviously vulnerable and the F.A.A. Observer School moved out leaving only a Ground School. The Luftwaffe carried out several attacks and one in May 1942 caused considerable damage to the F.A.A. base. Cunliffe Owen obtained a contract to convert Typhoons for operations from dust strips and about the same time were appointed sub-contractors by Westlands for building Seafire III's. Including Spitfires converted to Seafires a total of 350 were built, after which the line was altered to build later marks.

After the War Cunliffe Owen built a feeder airliner named the "Concordia" of which two were built. These aircraft failed to find a customer and as Cunliffe were now in financial difficulties they sold their plant to the Ford Motor Company and from which they now produce the Transit van.

Airlines using the airport in the post War period included B.U.A., Silver City, B.E.A., Jersey Airways, Manx, Air U.K., B.I.A., K.L.M.

A hard runway of 5,653 feet (1,723 metres) was opened in 1966.

In pre War days Eastleigh was a very successful airport, but the claim for passenger and aircraft movements must go to Portsmouth, whose figures were consistently higher. Examination of the numbers show that the latter city had the advantage of the Ryde ferry which at peak times operated up to twenty two flights per day with additional flights on demand and undoubtably this activity contributed significantly to Portsmouth's figures.

Southampton (Eastleigh) is now recognised as the regional airport in the South.

Bournemouth

The first recorded aviation event at Bournemouth was in July 1910 when an Aviation Week was held. This was the first time that British aviators competed in level terms with their Continental rivals; the British being represented by Grahame-White, Bertram Dickson, Robert Lorraine, A. Rawlinson and L.D. Gibbs, all flying Henry Farman biplanes. Other British pilots included W.D. McArdle and James Radley flying Bleriot monoplanes, C. Grace and G. Colmore in Short biplanes and finally A. Ogilvie and the Hon. C.S. Rolls with Wright biplanes, the former being built in France, while the mount of C.S. Rolls was built by Shorts. On the second day of the event C.S. Rolls was competing in a spot landing competition when he suffered structural

failure, and was killed in the subsequent crash.

After World War I Ensbury Park was used as a unlicenced landing ground and in 1919/20 Bournemouth Aviation Company operated up to five Avro 504's for joyriding. It is believed that they also operated a service to Weymouth but little is known about this. Ensbury Park stayed open until 1927 but, due to number of crashes, the local population made its feelings known to the Council who ordered it closed, its fate to become a housing estate.

In 1933 a new landing ground was opened at Somerford Bridge, but became universally known as Christchurch, the original occupants being Bournemouth Aero Club, but soon became a scheduled stop for a number of airlines. In 1934 Provincial Airlines called at Bournemouth on its Croydon - Plymouth service and this was followed on the 17th May by Western Airways on its Cardiff - Bristol - Bournemouth route, some of which connected with PSIOWA's service to Ryde thus offering a through ticket from Cardiff to the Island, and marketed jointly by both airlines as "Sunshine Air Express." In 1935 the landing ground was extended and thus became a properly constituted airport. The airport was officially opened an the 17th May by Countess Jellicoe who, accompanied by her daughter, Lady Prudence, flew from London in an Airspeed Courier of PSIOWA being welcomed by the Mayor of Christchurch, Norman Barnes, and Ryde, Major A. Dennis. Also present were Lionel Balfour, Managing Director of PSIOWA and his wife, Lady Myrtle *(nee Jellicoe)*. For part of 1935 Cobham Air Routes used Bournemouth as a Customs airport on its London - Guernsey route but this ceased when their Wessex G-ADEW ditched south of the Needles with the loss of the pilot.

In 1937 Channel Air Ferries extended its Shoreham - Isle of Wight service to Bournemouth and in the following year this service was further extended to various places in the West Country and continued until March 1939 when the route was taken over by Great Western and Southern Airlines. Subject to notice a flare path could be laid out. On the outbreak of war the airfield was requisitioned by the Air Ministry and used it as the support airfield for the radar establishment (later Royal Radar Establishment).

Christchurch became an important "junction" airport and between 1934 and 1939 it was used by the following airlines:-

Provincial Airlines	Cobham Air Routes,
Crilly Airways	Air Dispatch,
Channel Air Ferries	Railway Air Services,
Jersey Airways	PSIOWA,
Great Western and Southern Airlines	

Later on Christchurch was the main assembly base for Horsa gliders but this caused problems for the Whitleys when towing the gliders. The maximum run was 800 yards which ended in tall trees, but despite protests nothing was done until the crews refused to fly; this producing the desired result! Bournemouth *(Hurn)* was opened in 1943 and Christchurch was later closed, it now an Industrial Estate.

Shanklin (Apse)

Apse airfield was about one and a half miles from Shanklin and was opened in 1929 on land that was part of Apse Manor Farm which was owned by Mr and Mrs Fiske and in the summer of 1929 Inland Flying Services Ltd moved in from Maylands, near Romford. This company *(later re-named Wight Aviation Ltd and then PSIOWA)* was destined to become, by a very large margin, the most significant airline flying to the Island. They initially operated two Avro 504k's but in early 1930 they replaced one of these with DH 60X Moth G-AAAG powered by a 90hp Cirrus III and equipped with these two aircraft they formed the Island Flying Club, a wholly owned subsidiary. The Secretary was A.G. Murray, a solicitor who lived in Shanklin but is believed to have practiced in Portsmouth, the C.F.I. was W.E. Woodward who like A.G. Murray was also a director of the parent company. The club appears to have been reasonably well financed as a clubhouse was built and offered not only tea, coffee and snacks but was also licenced. One of the first pupils was a Charles Coombs, a charabanc and taxi owner who operated from his garage at Regent Street, Shanklin and was the first person on the Island to qualify for his "A" licence, subsequently putting this to good use at Languard Manor. To commemorate the official opening of the club an Air Pageant was held on the 20th June 1930 with Sir Alliott Verdon Roe officiating, displays were given by Moths, an Avro Avian, a Klemm 27A III and aerobatics by Lt. Col. L.A. Strange in a Spartan. The popularity of the event surprised even the organisers and, encouraged by this they arranged a second pageant which was held on the 17th August. It attracted some 8,000 spectators, the highlight being a fly past by 25 aircraft led by the Hon Mrs Victor Bruce flying a Bluebird. In 1932 PSIOWA started the first scheduled airline service to the Island but until Apse could be lengthened it was too small for the new Westland Wessex. PSIOWA did not, however, abandon Apse as services were operated by their Fox Moth and Puss Moth and later by Airspeed Couriers.

On the 9th July 1934 Sir Alan Cobham gave a display, one of the pilots being Geoffrey Tyson *(later to become Chief Test Pilot of Short Bros, and then Saro Ltd)* including an aerobatic display, parachute descents involving delayed drops, and Joan Meakin produced a spirited performance of aerobatics in her Rhonbussard glider. Sir Alan sent

twenty tickets for free flights to the Isle of Wight County Press who drew lots among the applicants, these tickets also including flights from Ryde where Sir Alan gave a display on the previous day.

By 1935 PSIOIWA operated the following routes into Apse:- Portsmouth - Ryde - Shanklin, Portsmouth - Shanklin direct, Southampton - Ryde - Shanklin, Shoreham - Ryde - Shanklin and finally London *(Heston)* - Ryde - Shanklin. It is uncertain as to when Apse closed but it was probably about the time that the new airport at Sandown *(Lea)* opened.

In February 1998 the hanger was still in existence.

Shanklin (Languard Manor)

Languard Manor was closer to Shanklin that Apse and consisted of a field surrounded by trees and hedges. The first person to qualify for a licence on the Island was Mr Charles Coombs who started Shanklin Flying Services at Languard in early 1931 with the intention of offering joyriding and taxi work. He bought three aircraft namely:- the prototype Spartan Arrow G-AAWY, the prototype Spartan Three Seater G-ABAZ named "Island Queen" and a Simmonds Spartan G-AAHA. Reports have suggested that G-ABAZ "Island Queen" had a red fuselage but this is only partly true as while owned by Coombs there is photographic evidence that the fuselage sides were a biscuit colour with a bluey-green decking and cowling. The colour scheme was probably changed to red in 1934/5 when it was bought by the Isle of Wight Flying Club. Coombs operated from Landguard for about three years but sold out to Mr E.H. Byrne. The latter gentleman was not satisfied with renting the field and constantly badgered the owner to sell him the land but the owner refused. Matters came to a head when Byrne threatened to leave, the response was a request to shut the gate behind him! Byrne then bought 161 acres of Lea Farm, Sandown which developed into a successful airport. Languard then reverted to agricultural use.

Hayling Island

A landing ground was first recorded in 1929 and was located south of the bridge with a landing run of 1,320 feet. It was initially used by Air Transport and Sales Ltd who also operated from landing grounds at Eastoke, Horndean and East Wittering. Their main function was joy riding, their aircraft being a Spartan and a Bluebird. By 1936 a hanger had been erected but prior to this Pauline Gower and Dorothy Spicer moved in and traded as Air Trips Ltd (believed 1934). Pauline concentrated on the flying and Dorothy on engineering offering servicing and overhaul work which made a significant contribution to their income.

Flying was mainly air taxi work and joy riding, some over to the Isle of Wight and by the end of 1936 their Spartan Three Seater G-ABKK "Helen of Troy" had carried over 25,000 passengers. Their partnership was amicably dissolved when they ceased operating in December 1936.

On the outbreak of War Pauline Gower became Commandant of the Air Transport Auxillary and in 1943 she was awarded the M.B.E. She became the first woman to be elected to the Board of British Airways but tragically died in childbirth in 1947 at the age of 36.

Dorothy Spicer completed her engineering studies and during the War worked at the R.A.E.Farnborough. Not long after the War she and her husband were killed in an air crash in South America.

Reverting to Hayling, the field was enlarged and used up to 1938 by the Hayling Island Flying Club.

Airspeed's factory at Portsmouth in 1937.   Credit: Portsmouth Public Record Office

Conclusion

Historically, pioneers rarely make money and the pre War internal airlines were no exception! In the 19th century the conversion from sail to steam produced a proliferation of shipping companies, many being just a one ship operation. The same principle applied to the railways with a multitude of regional companies who either went out of business or were swallowed up by more powerful rivals.

So it was with the internal airlines who sometimes made a profit in the odd year but nevertheless incurred substantial losses over the period from start up to the outbreak of war.

The far sighted Major General Sir Frederick Sykes, who in 1919 was appointed the first Director of Civil Aviation at the Air Ministry, stated at the end of that year "It may be questioned whether Civil Aviation in England is to be regarded as one of those industries which is unable to stand on its own feet, but is so essential to the national welfare that it must be kept alive at all costs." In March 1920 during a debate on the air estimates, Winston Churchill, who was both Minister of War and Air Minister, stated "Civil Aviation must fly by itself, the Government cannot possibly hold it up in the air."

The only subsidy granted was for airlines operating to the Continent and that was only because the Government was forced into a corner as British Airlines ceased operating because they could not compete with the heavily subsidised French. An argument could be constructed to the effect that as a result of the Government's attitude, British civil aviation failed to develop its full potential which contrasted heavily with the Germans and French who encouraged expansion. The latter kept a very watchful eye on the former and in order to create a large Air Force reserve they offered substantial subsidies. Under the Treaty of Versailles, the Germans were denied an Air Force, but airlines were encouraged not only by subsidies but various cities enticed them to operate to them by inducements such as the waiving of landing fees etc. By 1931 Germany had the largest route mileage in Europe at nearly three times that of the French. Comparative figures for 1931 being:-

	No of Transport Aircraft	Pilots Employed	Weekly Air Mileage
Germany	177	160	299,000
France	267	135	109,000
Italy	77	61	60,000

In the same year there were no British internal air routes whatsoever.

This lack of a growing air transport system obviously had an adverse effect on the manufacturers who were reluctant to commit resources to the design of an aircraft for a market that was virtually non existent, whereas the Germans had developed and were flying all metal Junkers monoplanes.

Other factors in the 1920's which mitigated against development was a lack of infrastructure, unsuitable aircraft, lack of finance, non existent navigational and radio aids, the competition from fast, reliable trains which travelled from and to city centres. The route structure, with few exceptions, was too short to compete effectively against the railways and therefore the only routes where the airlines had an advantage were those that operated over water. The independent airlines that survived until the outbreak of War all had over water routes, the principal ones being Mainland -Isle of Wight, Mainland - Channel Islands, Weston-Super-Mare - Cardiff, Blackpool - Isle of Man, Lands End - Scillies and the Scottish Island routes.

In the late 1920's and early 1930's aero engines were becoming not only more reliable, but more economic thus encouraging airframe manufacturers to design aircraft with lower operative costs than hitherto. Examples were the Westland Wessex, the de Havilland 84 Dragon and the Spartan Cruiser, the first two entering service in 1929 and the others in 1932 and 1933 respectively.

In 1928 wrote to all towns and cities with a population of over 20,000 pointing out the desirability of establishing municipal aerodromes. Given that civil aviation was controlled by a department of the Air Ministry, it is suspected that the motive was to obtain for "free" established landing grounds in the time of war. At that time France and not Germany was perceived to be the potential enemy and it is significant that by the early 1930's in the south and west the licenced airports were at Shoreham, Ryde, Portsmouth, Cowes, Southampton, Plymouth and Bristol, with the London area consisting of Croydon, Gatwick and Heston. In the country as a whole there were fifty eight aerodromes in 1931, but by 1935 had increased to ninety five. The problems of the airlines did not improve with the introduction of trains which were consistently capable of 100mph and whereas mainline stations were actually in the cities, aerodromes were obviously some distance outside thus the travelling time to and from the centre tended to nullify the advantage of air transport. Another factor was the extra cost which was approximately three times that of rail. In 1935 the average male earnings were 56/6 (£2.84) per week and therefore to undertake a return journey by air of two hundred miles each way would require seventy one hours earning time. The equivalent today would be in the region of sixteen hours. This cost put air transport out of the reach of the majority of citizens but to make matters worse was the very low utilisation achieved with aircraft only operating for an average of nineteen weeks in the year, which expressed another way, meant that they were idle for 64% of the time! Revenue might have been increased with the carriage of freight and the mails, but in respect of the former only a very limited amount could be carried and in regard to the mails, these were collected by the Post Office during the day and travelled to their destinations overnight, but the airlines did not fly after dark! This reduced their utilisation even further and as one observer remarked "Nobody will fly at night because there are no facilities and nobody will install facilities because there is no flying by night." Until 1939 when the Government subsidy became operative, there was no mandatory requirement to publish figures for passengers carried, mileage flown, load factors etc and it is considered that some airlines inflated their figures, the intention being to enhance their own importance. This did not apply to Railway Air Services as the railways had a policy of recording every little detail of their operations (no computers in those days). From commencement of operations in 1934 to 1938 Railway Air Services had an accumulated trading deficit of £192,545, this loss being accepted by the Board "For reasons of policy." Railway Air Services had the financial backing of the railways, but the independents were not in this fortunate position and it is estimated that most of them lost some 80% of their capital. It has been calculated that due to the low utilisation, a 100% load factor was required to break even but in reality the actual figure achieved was nearer an average of 35%, resulting in most of the independents suffering continued

losses. There were exceptions to this and, for example, in the first year of their operations, PSIOWA made a profit but this disappeared due to the decision to keep their staff on the payroll during the winter. They had a further advantage that their routes were over water and of short duration, thus increasing utilisation and at the same time competing effectively with the steamers. Usage was also increased by the popular "Round the Island" air cruise and by various charters but despite this it is unlikely that they ever made an operating profit.

The South Coast airports were very active and the figures were:

		Bournemouth	Southampton	Portsmouth	Shoreham
1935	**Aircraft movements**	2,658	6,799	10,773	1,018
	Passengers	4,386	21,170	24,974	1,197
1936	**Aircraft movements**	*Not available*	5,288	9,044	1,022
	Passengers	*Not available*	24,606	25,385	2,918

On the Island Ryde rapidly became the principal airport and the figures show that, in terms of movements and passenger throughput, Ryde was on a par with Portsmouth and Southampton. With the exception of Croydon and Heston, which were the main airports for overseas flights, the two South Coast cities plus Ryde were the three busiest airports in the Country. This is indicative of the population in the South more readily embracing air transport than the rest of the Country and is further accounted for by higher incomes combined with the high density route structure.

We now come to the policy of the railways and through them Railway Air Services/Great Western and Southern Airlines. Their activities demonstrated that they were predatory, and indeed, it would have been out of character if they were not. A cursory examination of the history of the railways shows that they forced the canals out of business, swallowed the weaker railways, took over and developed the ferry routes to the Continent and Ireland and then proceeded to establish or take over coach and road haulage companies. When the Southern Railway acquired what amounted to a controlling interest in the Isle of Wight Bus Company, Southern Vectis then went on to swallow the remaining ten Island independent bus operators, thereby creating a monopoly of surface transport. Their policy of gaining control was not the modern "smash and grab" technique but one of stealth whereby they would invest up to 49% of a company which, because of their marketing and ticketing strengths, would effectively control the company. The railways could afford to be patient as the "victim" company would have to stand their share of the losses.

The railways only competitor with any financial strength was Whitehall Securities Corporation Ltd who owned a number of airlines including Spartan, all of which were amalgamated to form British Airways. It has not gone unnoticed that their Managing Director, the Hon Clive Pearson, was also a Director of the Southern Railway! British Airways progressively developed Continental and Scandinavian routes and while Railway Air Services showed no inclination to do likewise, one wonders if there was some form of tacit agreement between them. Another indication of the railways protectionism was the banning of all travel agents who dealt with other airlines and by the beginning of 1939 they had stakes in Jersey Airways, Great Western and Southern Airlines, the Olley Group and by the middle of the War they had acquired 100% of all these companies. This left only one competitor on the Isle of Wight routes, namely PSIOWA. In 1944 the railways and PSIOWA submitted a proposal for post War air services and this was approved by Lord Swinton. Due to the election of a Labour Government, these plans never materialised but had they done so there is little doubt that PSIOWA would have been absorbed into Railway Air Services.

The practice of the railways was not necessarily bad as it brought some discipline into a very fragmented, underfunded industry and they therefore eliminated wasteful competition and set in motion the basic structure upon which to expand. There is no doubt that at the cost of a little under £200,000 they gained a wealth of operating experience which would have stood them in good stead had they been allowed to continue after the War.

All the operators were, in the full sense of the word, pioneers and plunged into a new and unknown business with all the attendant pitfalls that are constantly present in such an enterprise. Despite Government indifference and even when faced with continuing losses, they never lost faith and for this they must be commended.

Post War services to the Isle of Wight were very fragmentary and never reached anything like the pre War level. They were mainly weekend operations using Dragon Rapides, Dakotas and Herons. The companies failed to pay sufficient attention to market research and like the railways in the 1920's failed to see the advance of the private motor vehicle. In 1937 at the zenith of air services to the Island, only one person in twenty six owned a car but by 1970 this figure was one in nine, and ten years later in 1980 it was down to one in four. The two shipping companies, British Rail and Red Funnel, took this very seriously and commissioned the construction of purpose built Ro-Ro car ferries and at the time of writing there are seven modern car ferries operating out of Portsmouth and Southampton, each with a capacity of some 140 cars.

Is there a future for air transport to the Island? The answer is yes, but not from the U.K. market.

In recent years the number of foreign visitors to the Island have steadily increased, the main influx being from Holland, Germany, Denmark and Sweden. Those from Scandinavia have a 24 hour sea journey and then have to drive from Harwich, while visitors from other Northern European countries have a lengthy drive before boarding a ferry in France, all this cutting into holiday time.

It is considered that the Island should be marketed in those countries as a "Microcosm of England" offering rolling downs and hills, good beaches, stately buildings and traditional villages. Ramblers should not be overlooked as the Island offers many miles of footpaths with panoramic views. The various sectors of the tourist industry in the Island, such as hotels, coach firms, car hire companies etc should co-operate to put together and offer package deals to those Continental visitors. This could easily be done with the willing help of airlines from the countries concerned.

Bembridge Airport with its hard runway could accept modern aircraft and requires very little additional expenditure. This would undoubtably produce the usual emotive protests of aircraft noise but this does not stand up to objective assessment. All commercial aircraft have to pass strict noise limitations which are far below that of diesel trucks which are not only very noisy, but emit noxious fumes.

The market is there and it only requires the will to capitalise on it with the consequent benefit to the economy of the Island.

Finally, without the dedication of the pioneers, Britain would have been the only major country to emerge from the Second World War with no experience of internal air transport whatsoever.

OLLEY AIR SERVICE, LTD.

GENERAL OFFICES—AIRPORT OF LONDON CROYDON ENGLAND, TEL.: CROYDON 5117; TELEGRAMS: 'FLYOLLEY', PHONE CROYDON

Main Agents in the British Isles for the Following Associated Companies

IRISH SEA AIRWAYS (operated jointly by West Coast Air Services and Aer Lingus Teoranta) and
CHANNEL AIR FERRIES LIMITED

IRISH SEA AIRWAYS
London-Bristol-Dublin

	Daily	excpt Sun.	**75** To Oct. 1st	excpt Sun.	Daily		
	AM	PM		AM	PM		
	10 00	5 00	Lv...LONDON...Ar	11 30	5 00		
	11 00	6 00	Lv...BRISTOL...Lv	10 30	4 00		
	12 45	7 45	Ar...DUBLIN...Lv	9 00	2 30		
	PM	PM		AM	PM		

Dublin—Isle of Man

	excpt Sun.	excpt Sun.	**76** To Sept. 19	excpt Sun.	excpt Sun.		
	AM	PM		PM	PM		
	9 05	1 30	Lv...DUBLIN...Ar	12 30	3 45		
	10 05	2 30	Ar.ISLE OF MAN.Lv	11 30	2 45		
	AM	PM		AM	PM		

Fares

£	One Way	60 Day Round Trip	15 Day Round Trip	7 Day Excursion	Excess Baggage
London-Dublin........	5.10.0	10. 0.0	9. 0.0	7.7.0	1/-per kilo
Bristol-Dublin........	3.10.0	6.10.0	—	—	1/-per kilo
Dublin-Isle of Man.....	1.10.0	2.15.0	2.10.0	—	6d. per kilo

Free baggage allowance 15 kilo (33 lbs.) per passenger.

WORLD WIDE CHARTER SERVICE

NIGHT AND DAY
to
ANYWHERE
from
LONDON

—— CHARTER AIR LINES

Our Charter Service is considered to be the FINEST in Europe, our Pilots, Personnel, and Equipment are the most UP TO DATE in the British Isles.

OUR SLOGAN—Anywhere, Anytime, is lived up to, and our ORGANIZATION is so complete that NIGHT and day we are available to FLY YOU ANYWHERE at a MOMENT'S NOTICE.

Special Notice to United States Visitors to Great Britain: Let us arrange a FLYING ITINERARY for you. Communicate with us and we will mail you a reply immediately.

CHERBOURG—LONDON

We can pick you up from your LINER AT CHERBOURG and have you in LONDON 1¼ hours LATER. . . . A saving of 12 hours' sea and train journey.

LONDON (Croydon)—Telephone Croydon 5117-8-9; Telegrams, 'FLYOLLEY', phone Croydon 5117-8-9, Day or Night.
NEW YORK (Brooklyn)—O. J. Whitney, Inc., Floyd Bennett Airport, Telephone ESplanada 7-5600; Telegrams, 'OJWINC', New York.

CHANNEL AIR FERRIES
London-Isle of Wight; Brighton-Bristol-Cardiff

excpt Tues.	*excpt Tues.	excpt Tues.	excpt Tues.	**77** To Oct. 1st	excpt Tues.	excpt Tues.	excpt Tues.	*excpt Tues.
PM	PM	PM	AM		PM	PM	PM	PM
	3 15			Lv..HESTON..Ar				8 30
	3 40			Lv..LONDON..Lv				8 05
4 00	—	1 45	8 30	Lv.BRIGHTON.Ar	12 30	3 35	7 50	—
4 25	4 20	2 10	8 55	Ar.ISLE OF WIGHT Lv	12 10	3 15	7 30	7 35
4 35		2 20	9 05	Lv.ISLE OF WIGHT Ar	12 00	3 05	7 20	
4 50		2 35	9 20	Ar..Bournemouth..Lv	11 45	2 50	7 05	
5 00			9 30	Ar..Bournemouth..Ar	11 35		6 55	
5 40			10 10	Lv...BRISTOL...Lv	11 05		6 25	
5 55			10 25	Ar...CARDIFF...Lv	10 40		6 00	
PM	PM	PM	AM		AM	PM	PM	PM

*—Daily except Tuesdays (by request).

Fares

£	Bournemouth	Brighton	Bristol	Cardiff	Heston	Isle of Wight	London
Bournemouth....	....	1. 2.0 2. 1.6	1. 0.0 1.15.0	1. 9.6 2.12.6	1.19.6 3. 9.0	0. 9.0 0.17.6	1.14.6 2.19.6
Brighton........	1. 2.0 2. 1.6	....	1.14.0 3. 2.6	2. 1.0 3.15.0	....	0.13.0 1. 4.0	....
Bristol........	1. 0.0 1.15.0	1.14.0 3. 2.6	....	0. 9.6 0.17.6	2.19.6 5. 4.0	1. 7.6 2. 5.0	2.14.6 4.14.6
Cardiff........	1. 9.6 2.12.6	2. 1.0 3.15.0	0. 9.6 0.17.6	....	3. 9.0 6. 1.6	1.15.0 3. 0.0	3. 4.0 5.12.0
Heston........	1.19.6 3. 9.0	....	2.19.6 5. 4.0	3. 9.0 6. 1.6	....	1.10.6 2.15.0	0. 7.6 0.13.6
Isle of Wight....	0. 9.0 0.17.6	0.13.0 1. 4.0	1. 7.6 2. 5.0	1.15.0 3. 0.0	1.10.6 2.15.0	....	1. 5.6 2. 4.6
London........	1.14.6 2.19.6	....	2.14.6 4.14.6	3. 4.0 5.12.0	0. 7.6 0.13.6	1. 5.6 2. 4.6	....

6d. kilo between all airports. Free baggage allowance 15 kilo (33 lbs.) per passenger.

London-Luxembourg

	Wed. only	**78**	Fri. only	
	AM		PM	
	8 30	Lv...LONDON...Ar	2 45	
	11 00	Ar LUXEMBOURG Lv	11 45	
	AM		AM	

FARE—London-Luxembourg; One way £5.10.0; 15 day round trip £9.10.0; 60 day round trip £10.0.0.
EXCESS BAGGAGE: 1/-per kilo. Free baggage allowance 15 kilo (33 lbs.) per passenger.
Sterling equivalent in Lux Francs.

Plymouth-Penzance-Isle of Scilly

(a) excpt Sun.	(b) excpt Sun.	Sun. Only	excpt Sun.	excpt Sun.	**79**	excpt Sun.	excpt Sun.	Sun. Only	(b) excpt Sun.	(a) excpt Sun.
PM	PM	PM	AM	AM		AM	AM	PM	PM	PM
			11 25		Lv..PLYMOUTH..Ar		10 25			
			12 15		Ar..PENZANCE..Lv		9 35			
7 00	6 00	12 30		8 30	Lv..PENZANCE..Ar	9 20		1 20	6 50	7 50
7 20	6 20	12 50		8 50	Ar.ISLE OF SCILLY Lv	9 00		1 00	6 30	7 30
PM	PM	PM		AM		AM		PM	PM	PM

(a)—Service summer only till Sept. 10th and on Sunday by request.
(b)—Until October 1, 1938.

Fares

Plymouth-Penzance—One way £1.5.0; Round trip £2.4.0. Excess Baggage 6d. per kilo.
Plymouth-Isle of Scilly—One way £2.5.0; Round Trip £3.19.0. Excess Baggage 6d. per kilo.
Isle of Scilly-Penzance—One way £1.0.0; Round trip £1.15.0. Excess Baggage 4d. per kilo.

Free Baggage allowance 12 kilo (25 lbs.) per passenger.

Bibliography

Airspeed Aircraft since 1931   HA Taylor
Putnams 1970

Airspeed, the Company and its Aeroplanes DH Middleton
Terrence Dalton 1992

A Million Miles in the Air   Gordon Olley
Hodder & Stoughton 1934

Annals of British Aviation 1919-1960   John Stroud
Putnams 1962

Avro Aircraft since 1908   AJ Jackson
Putnams 1965

British Aviation. Ominous Skies 1935-1939 Harald Penrose
HMSO

British Aviation. The Pioneer Years   Harald Penrose
Cassell 1966

British Aviation. Widening Horizons 1930-1934 *Harald Penrose*
HMSO

British Civil Aircraft 1919-1972   AJ Jackson Vols I, II, III
Putnams 1973

British Historical Statistics   BR Mitchell
Cambridge University Press 1988

British Piston Aero Engines   A Lumsden
Airlife 1996

British Transport   HJ Dyos & DH Aldcroft
Leicester University Press 1971

de Havilland Aircraft since 1909   AJ Jackson
Putnams 1978

Fifty Years Fly Past   Geoffrey Dorman
Forbes Robertson 1951

Hampshire Airfields of World War II   RJ Brooks
Countryside Books 1996

Herbert Walker's (Sir) Southern Railway CF Klapper
Ian Allan 1973

History of British Aviation
1908-1914 Vols I & II   R Dallas Brett 1933
Republished as one volume 1988
by Air Research

History of the Southern Railway   Michael Bonavia
Unwin Hyman 1987

History of the World Airlines   REG Davis
Oxford University Press 1967

Imperial Airways and the
First British Airlines 1919-1940   AS Jackson
Terrence Dalton 1995

Industrial Archaeology in the   Allan Insole
Isle of Wight   & Alan Parker
Isle of Wight County Council 1979

Knights of the Air   Peter King
Constable & Company Ltd

Peaceful Fields   JF Hamlin
GMS Enterprises 1996

Pigs Wings and Other Things   WH Llewellyn
1989

Portsmouth City Council Minutes of the Docks and Airport Committee
1930-1939

Reports on the Progress of
British Civil Aviation 1932-1939   Air Ministry
HMSO

Railway Air Services   John Stroud
Ian Allan 1967

Rebel Airman. Biography of
Lt. Col. Louis Strange   Peter Hearn
HMSO 1994

Sandown. An Island's Airport   K Davies
HPC Publishing 1992

Saunders Roe and SARO Aircraft   Peter London
Putnams 1988

"Sea to Air". History of Saunders Roe RL Wheeler & AE Tagg
Crossprint 1989

Sea Eagle to Flamingo
- History of Jersey Airlines   Neville Doyle
Self Publishing Association 1992

Shoreham Airport, Sussex   TMA Webb & DL Bird
Cirrus Associates 1996

Sky Fever   Sir Geoffrey de Havilland
Hamish Hamilton 1961

Solent Flight   IJ Hilliker
Kingfisher Publications 1990

Somewhere in the West Country   Ken Wakefield
Crécy Publishing Ltd

Southampton Corporation.
Minutes of the Airport Committee 1934 - 1939

Southern Vectis. The First 60 Years   R Newman
Ensign Publications

Solent Sky   Peter T New

Studies in British Transport
History 1870 - 1970   DH Aldcroft
Scottish Journal of Political Economy No: 12 1965

The Brabazon Story   Lord Brabazon of Tara
William Heineman 1956

The Story of the British Light Aeroplane John Murray
Terence Boughton 1963

To the Sunset Bound   MJ Ingram
Air Britain 1987

Supermarine Aircraft since 1914   CF Andrews
Putnams 1981   & LEB Morgan

Transport on the Isle of Wight

Wight Aircraft. The Aircraft of
J Samuel White Ltd, Cowes   Mike Goodall
Gentry Books 1973

Wings over Westminster   Harold Balfour
Hutchinsons 1973   (Lord Balfour of Inchrye)

Wings across the World   Harald Penrose
Cassell & Company Ltd 1980

Portsmouth Aerocar on flypast at SBAC show, Radlett 1947.   Credit: Portsmouth Aviation

Replica Boxkite

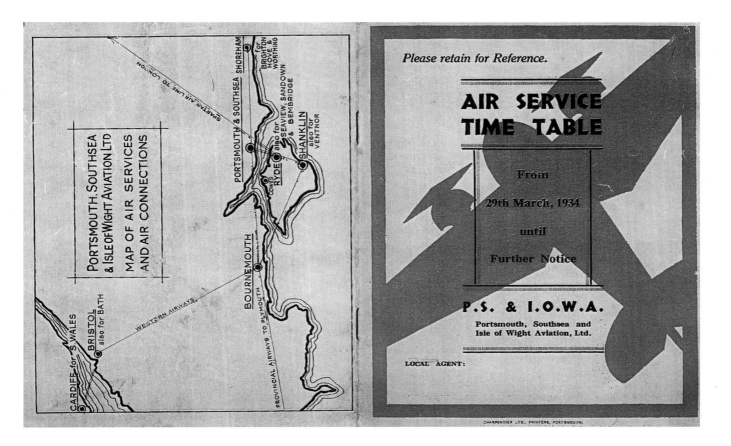

WESTLAND "WESSEX".

3-140 H.P. ARMSTRONG SIDDELEY 7 CYL.8 "GENET-MAJOR" ENGINES.

THIS "WESSEX" WAS DOPED SILVER ALL OVER DURING TEST FLIGHTS.

1932

PSIOWA stamps

Credit: Charles Taylor

Medallions struck to commemorate the opening of Bristol Whitchurch

Credit: Mike Tozer

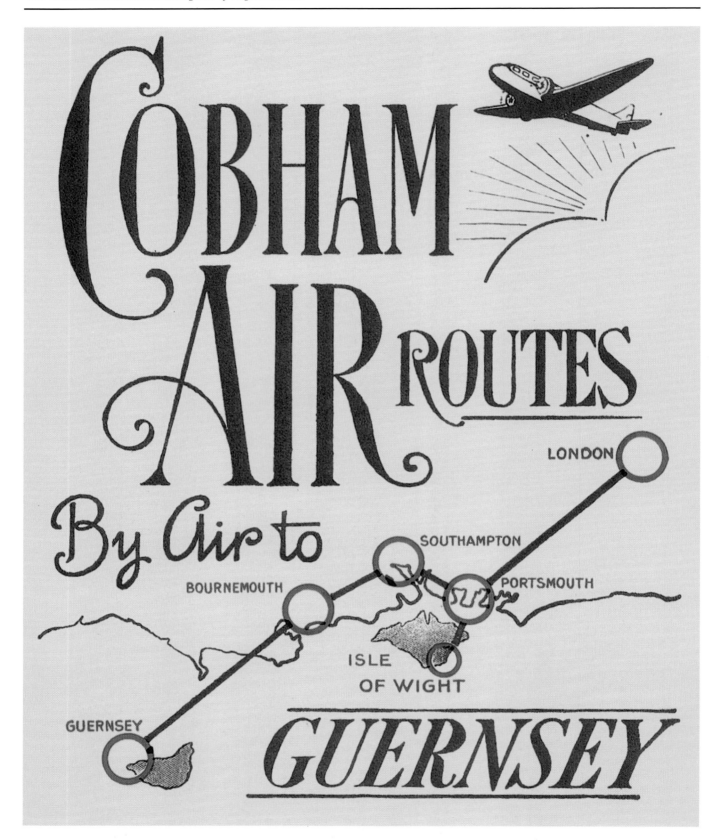

1935

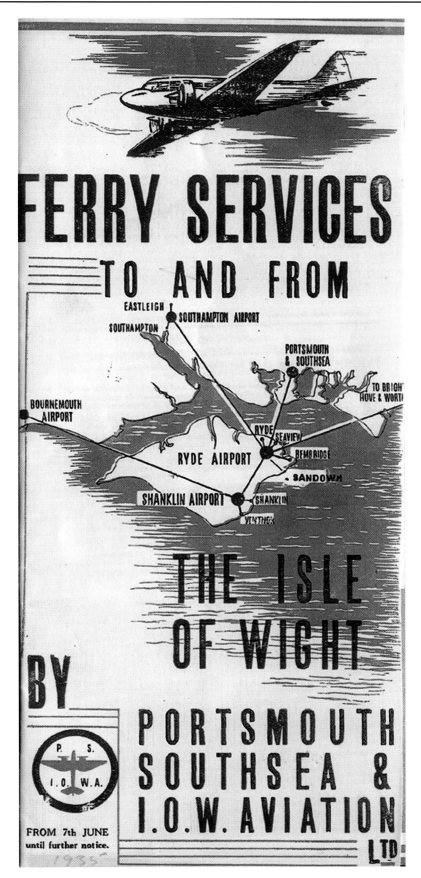

1935

Credit: Charles Taylor

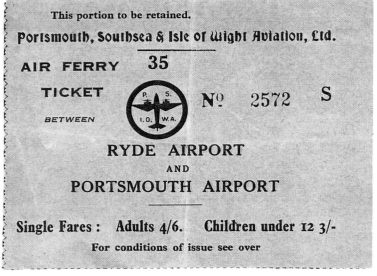

Credit: Charles Taylor

SOUTHAMPTON
MUNICIPAL
AIRPORT
1939

ITS SERVICES AND FACILITIES

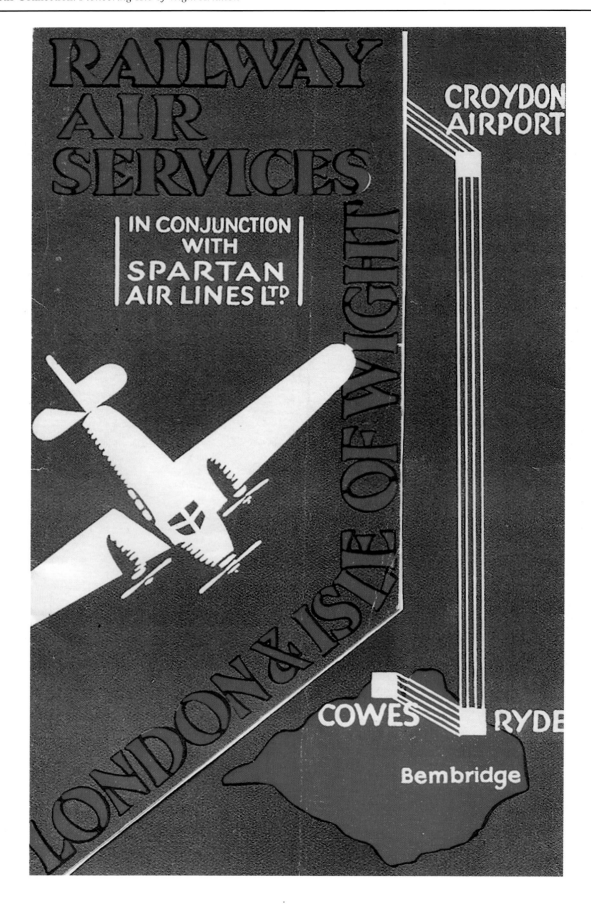

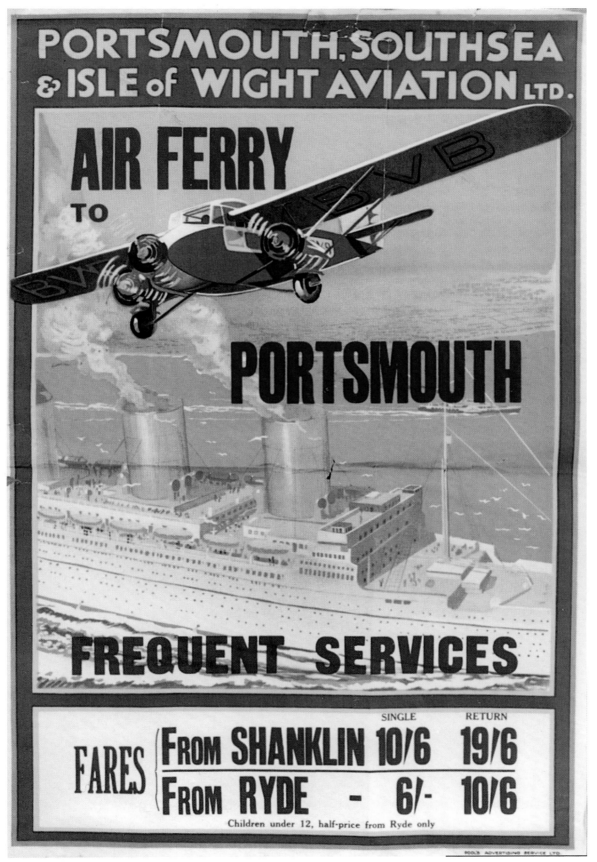

Credit: Chris Balfour

The Beehive, Gatwick

Credit: John King